D0498145

WITHDRAWN
UTSA LIBRARIES

From Customer Retention to a Holistic Stakeholder Management System

Margit Huber · Susanne O'Gorman

From Customer Retention to a Holistic Stakeholder Management System

Living a Vision

 Springer

Dr. Margit Huber
Dr. Susanne O'Gorman

TNS Infratest GmbH
Landsberger Straße 338
80687 München
Germany

margit.huber@tns-infratest.com
susanne.ogorman@tns-infratest.com

ISBN 978-3-540-77429-7   e-ISBN 978-3-540-77430-3

DOI 10.1007/978-3-540-77430-3

Library of Congress Control Number: 2007943073

ⓒ 2008 Springer-Verlag Berlin Heidelberg

Production: LE-TEX Jelonek, Schmidt & Vöckler GbR, Leipzig
Cover design: WMX Design GmbH, Heidelberg

Printed on acid-free paper

9 8 7 6 5 4 3 2 1

springer.com

Dedicated to Jo Scharioth

(the founder of TRI*M)

Introduction

The Emerging Market of Stakeholder Management

Margit Huber

About 20 years ago the term Stakeholder Management was very rarely used by managers as their main focus at that time was either on product quality or at more mature companies business reengineering.

When stakeholders were to be considered the first thing which came into mind at that time were customers. In the early 80s, leading players in the global market acknowledged the importance of their customers for the success of their business. As a consequence first companies – at that time mainly in the US – started to measure customer satisfaction. This idea of quality management was endeavoured by the Malcolm Baldrige National Quality Award in the US.

This can be considered as the foundation of a new area within market research challenging the leading marketing information companies to come up with analytical instruments to measure customer satisfaction and provide business insights allowing managers to better understand the existing customer base.
In Europe this American trend was observed carefully. The customer satisfaction business was considered to be the fastest growing sector within the market research industry globally.

An innovative and midterm oriented market research company like Infratest identified customer satisfaction as a (future) competitive advantage for the market research industry. Therefore, the time was ripe to look for a research solution which could be applied across many geographies as well as industries. Infratest Management made the strategic decision to invest in this area by either acquiring an existing tool or developing its own system. Jo Scharioth was mandated to look after this business and the first thing he initiated, was to carry out a feasibility study which should provide input for either developing or acquiring a solution. It very quickly turned out that the existing approaches – of which the Walker methodology at that time was the leading one – were not really what the company was looking for. Consequently management took the risk to make significant investments in this market by developing its own research product.

As Infratest was meanwhile commissioned with various customer satisfaction programmes it was of utmost importance to develop an approach based on a common philosophy. The underlying idea was to help our customers across all industries and markets to measure customer satisfaction in a consistent but at the same time highly customised way. Furthermore the probably most genius idea at that time was to create an offering which is not only applicable to customers as one stakeholder group but to any other constituency a company has to interact with. This gave us the unique chance to differentiate in the marketplace from the very beginning.

The general idea of a fact based management system which comprises the Measuring, Managing and Monitoring aspects finally led to the product name TRI*M which was to be the starting point of a long-term success story.

The first challenge was to develop the methodological basics of TRI*M – a massive challenge in a world of market researchers who all had substantial experience in how to best measure customer satisfaction. Besides there was extensive effort needed to convince the market research community that the time was ripe for what is today called a branded product or business solution. The aim was to create a conceptually simple yet sophisticated approach which should be applicable for any company interested in increasing their customer satisfaction.

This led to extensive discussions whether customer satisfaction or retention should be the main objective for a company and how this would impact the underlying analytical model. It was a perpetual process of elaborating ideas, defining preconditions, reworking the initial model, drafting diagrams and running various analyses on existing data. Ian Jarvis is addressing the creation of the model in more detail in his article on "The Beginnings of TRI*M".

There were mainly two features which made the TRI*M offering superior in the market place from the very beginning. One was the insight that the Index needs to reflect more than customer satisfaction. Companies that want to satisfy their current customer base and survive in the market place in the long run need to understand to what extent they are able to retain their existing customers. For that reason the fourth TRI*M Index question which deals with the perceived competitive advantage of a company was the decisive one. Having applied this question for nearly 20 years to several million interviews in thousands of surveys we see that this question is not only sensitive to market situations with different levels of expectation,, but also works as an early warning indicator. From our Benchmarking Database we clearly see that it is the toughest challenge for companies to gain competitive advantage with their products and services offered regarding customer retention. Susanne O'Gorman gives more insight into our general learning from the four Index questions and specific industry challenges in her article about TNS' Experience Database.

The second deliverable of the initial product offering was the key driver analysis which is unique because of its three dimensional approach. As TRI*M was designed from the very beginning to be a top management information system with high actionability there was the need to develop a graph which could show the key drivers of a company's customer retention at one glance. This led to a matrix which does not only differentiate between stated and derived importance but also reflects the performance of a company on each single attribute. To be able to deliver this information to senior management differentiation was made between those aspects which drive customer retention significantly – the so-called Motivators – and those which are only Hidden Opportunities, meaning that they have a high influence on customer retention but are not "top of mind" at present. Besides there are two areas which do not have an equally high impact on customer retention, namely Hygiene Factors and Potentials/Savers. Whereas Hygienics need to be observed as they are talked about quite frequently there is no immediate need to deliver above average on them. The fourth area comprises either attributes where costs can be saved without harming the existing level of customer retention (Savers) or in case of new product features or services offered, they can be deployed as Potentials for future drivers of customer retention.

Why the TRI*M Grid analysis is still superior to many other approaches offered in the market research industry is explained in more detail in Ian Jarvis' article as well as in many other articles from practitioners either in this book or in one of the three previous volumes we have published on the topic of Stakeholder Management.

When Jones and Sasser of Harvard Business school published their article on different types of loyalty, this perfectly matched with the customer retention approach of TRI*M. Based on their insight the four customer types a company has to typically deal with we have developed the TRI*M typology. With this we could provide our clients a better understanding of their customer base. From then on we were able to tell whether a company is facing a more satisfaction or loyalty driven customer relationship. Furthermore based on the TRI*M Typology we are able to calculate the so-called market resistance ratio which puts more meaning behind the Word-of-Mouth Management. For more information on the Customer Typology and their development over time see also Susanne O'Gorman's article.

Apart from understanding the key drivers of customer retention of one's own corporation it is also important to know in respect of gaining market shares how competitors are perceived from the customer's point of view. Together with a client of ours we were able to develop a further unique deliverable of TRI*M which was the competitive analysis. The management information provided with this tool is the insight in unique selling propositions which can be translated and embedded later on into marketing actions.

As mentioned above TRI*M as a research product was developed almost 20 years ago to respond to the increasing demand for customer satisfaction insights in the market research industry. Since then many developments and innovations have been made based on the core philosophy set out above. The huge success of the TRI*M system in the market research world combined with the globalisation of market research companies as such, the experience base we could build on was growing vastly. As Infratest as the owner of the TRI*M system was undergoing several mergers and acquisitions in the past decade TRI*M had the potential for rapid growth. However, this went hand in hand with a growing demand for innovation and expert advice from client side.

One of the latest developments is the process and execution analysis which allows a company to understand how consistent they deliver their products and services and to what extent they need to adjust their processes in achieving better customer retention.

As TRI*M strives with all its analytical tools to enable companies to take immediate actions for improving their stakeholder relationships, the implementation process is similarly important as the survey design and execution. For that reason it is crucial for an organisation to have the management buy-in for such an effort from the very beginning – not only to assure the success of the survey itself but to embed a customer survey programme in the company strategy. The MAN case study in this book shows very well how a successful customer satisfaction programme was set up from the very beginning in this company and how individual research need from specific business units are met in the same way than the overall management requirement for the strategic objective of customer orientation.

In many companies the strategic importance of Stakeholder Research is underlined by incorporating survey results into Company Scorecards. In many companies we work closely with project and process owners not only to derive appropriate actions from TRI*M Grid results but also to develop appropriate Key Performance Indicators which are used for target setting. Several articles within this book elaborate on how this is being done in various companies.

As said earlier, the TRI*M philosophy from the very beginning was based to go beyond customer retention. As the general approach allowed surveying all stakeholder groups of a company we always paid attention to transfer our learnings to any stakeholder group besides customers. It is obvious that there is a strong correlation between satisfied employees and satisfied clients. Many companies do research on both. Based on the vast experience we have from a great amount of multinational employee surveys, we are able not only to provide actionable insight for our clients regarding the driving factors of their employees' commitment but also can offer Benchmarks for many regions of the world. The case study of Evonik Industries shows very well how an employee survey helped them to accompany an integration process and company development. The article outlines how the analytical tools of TRI*M Employee Commitment were deployed to understand the overall company situation as well as it helped to gain insights on challenges in specific countries and business units. For those who are interested in how a bank uses the instrument to manage its Human Resources for the long-term business success, there is a specific article to be found within this book.

It goes without saying that TRI*M would not be a widely accepted management tool and thus the market leader in Stakeholder Management worldwide, if there was no validation for the results provided. The often raised question whether there is a pay-off for the research spending or – put in other words – "what is the ROI of customer retention or employee commitment investments?" is something we are constantly challenged with. Based on the many programmes we have been commissioned with in the past years we had the possibility to constantly validate our data. The most convincing way of doing this is by linking our data to business results of our clients. However, this is a process of confidence as business data needs to be provided to the research vendor. As TNS has with many key clients a long-lasting and trustworthy customer relationship we are provided with sensible business data by many clients. In linkage analyses we often find clear correlations e.g. between TRI*M Indices and defection rates or the business performance of specific branches.

The title of the book – From Customer Retention to a Holistic Stakeholder Management System – is also reflected in the choice of articles. Ian Jarvis gives evidence of the early days of TRI*M and shows in his article how TRI*M has been set up as a Customer Retention System. Some of the companies portrayed in this publication have accompanied the move from TRI*M Customer Retention to a holistic Stakeholder Management System since its very beginnings. Messe München has been measuring the satisfaction with its trade fairs since 1995 and also Commerzbank and Degussa are examples of long-term TRI*M clients whom we have shared many valuable experiences with. On the other hand, UNITE is an example of a relatively new TRI*M client who is planning to apply a 360° Stakeholder Management Approach which integrates customers, employees, internal processes and also business partners – thus moving towards a holistic Stakeholder Management System.

Apart from some examples mentioned above, this book comprises manifold insights into Stakeholder Management from colleagues who have contributed articles on specific topics as well as from practitioners who share their experiences with TRI*M publicly.

The valued reader of this book will find aspects covered such as

- how to design a specific customer retention programme with the help of a discovery workshop
- reporting needs for different target audiences in a company
- how to translate research findings into actions through implementation workshops
- why managing the employee commitment is similarly important in an organisation as customer satisfaction or
- how Stakeholder Management is applied to the Public sector.

I would like to especially thank all the TNS colleagues who have contributed their leisure time to make this book happen and all clients who have managed to cut out time apart from their daily work for putting down their experiences with Stakeholder Management Research. Apart from this, the fourth edition of our book would not have been possible without the continuous dedication of Martina Pallas to this project which comprises the constant encouragement of the authors to meeting the deadlines as well as the supervision of translations, proofreading and preparation of the layout for printing.

Apart from offering various case studies, this book is to honour **Jo Scharioth**, the founder of the TRI*M System. One intention of this book is to prove how he made it possible to **T**urn **R**ough **I**deas into a **M**anagement tool – which just is one other possibility of explaining the meaning of the word TRI*M.

He has not only dedicated his vast knowledge on Stakeholder Management to make this business solution the leading tool in the market research world and thus contributed significantly to the success of TNS today. We are looking at a significant market share of Stakeholder Management globally and still see above average growth in this arena as a market research corporation.

Jo is a living compendium of Stakeholder Management Research, impressively patient in explaining the tool to every single person over many years – no matter of what hierarchical level – who was willing to learn about TRI*M. We may need to revert to this knowledge source from time to time when we – as his scholars – come to boundaries he never found hindering but as a challenge for his unlimited passion and admirable energy to constantly innovate and drive the success of TRI*M. "Living a vision" has always been the driving force for Jo Scharioth which makes him a passionate and restless ambassador for TRI*M and the whole topic of Stakeholder Management.

Dear Jo Scharioth we – all the authors who have contributed to this book and many more TRI*M Apostles you have created throughout the organisation as well as on the client side over the past 20 years – would like to thank you for all the knowledge you shared with us in a selfless and inspiring way at any time.

We are aware on the valuable heritage you leave behind and hope to build on this foundation for the future success of our Stakeholder Management Area of Expertise.

Contents

1 The Beginnings of TRI*M – a Personal Account

Ian Jarvis

For those of us who work with TRI*M every day, in some cases for many years, it is perhaps difficult to imagine a world without TRI*M! It is just there, and seems to have been there for ever – although, of course, it didn't exist until Jo Scharioth invented it nearly 20 years ago.

We take for granted the TRI*M Index, the TRI*M Grid and the other TRI*M tools that have been developed since. And we take for granted that they are as they are – that the Index is an index, and not some other form of measure; that it is a composite of the four key questions that measure retention 'in the round', rather than being based on a single satisfaction/retention question or some other set of questions; that the Grid shows both Stated Importance and Calculated Importance (Impact on Retention), and not just one or the other; that these two measures of Importance, and quality element performance, are shown in relative and not absolute terms; and so on.

Most of us know why the TRI*M tools are constructed as they are and it all seems so obvious – but it wasn't at all obvious when Jo sat down with a blank sheet of paper back in 1989.

1.1 A Little Bit of (Infratest-Burke) Corporate History

Infratest acquired the European operations of the US firm Burke Marketing Research in 1980.

The two businesses were very different. Infratest was a, if not the, dominating force in the German market; the Burke operations were second or even third tier in their respective countries. Infratest was organised by market sector, with specialist businesses servicing different markets – Automotive, Finance, Health, IT/Telecoms, etc; Burke was primarily a consumer, FMCG research company. And the research cultures were different, with Infratest being more European/statistically oriented and Burke being more American/pragmatically orientated.

And finally, of course, the Infratest operations were nearly all located together in Munich, whereas the Burke operations were scattered across five countries.

In the mid-1980s, the Board set up the FAST Group ('Future Allied Strategy Team') with, as the name implies, the brief of recommending ways of leveraging strengths in one part of the company for the benefit of the group as a whole, and of integrating the Infratest and Burke businesses.

One conclusion of the FAST Group's deliberations was that it was easier to transfer **product** knowledge / expertise from one company to another than it was to transfer industry **sector** knowledge. The model we had here was the BASES simulated test market product which Burke Europe offered under licence from Burke USA at the time: it had proved relatively easy to train people on the BASES system in different countries (and to provide a centre of excellence to support them with analysis and consulting services); but it had proved more difficult to train people how to do Financial research or Health research, for example, when they didn't have at least a modicum of experience in the field (and client credibility!) to start with. So, one way of bringing the companies together – admittedly easier said than done – was to develop research products that all companies could offer in their individual market places.

Another outcome from the FAST Group's activities was an analysis of the existing business by type of research (product research, advertising research, U&A/market description studies, etc), from which it emerged that some 20% of our business was customer satisfaction research of one sort or another, which at the time was the fastest growing sector in the market research business world-wide. The trouble was that, whenever we were commissioned to carry out a CS study, we treated it as an ad hoc project and 're-invented the wheel' each time; or alternatively just implemented the client's standard CS programme. We had no CS philosophy of our own, let alone anything approaching a product.

1.2   Enter Jo Scharioth

Jo's arrival at Infratest was as much fortuitous as it was any direct result of the FAST Group's recommendations, but either way it was at least consistent with them. Jo had been a consultant with the Battelle Institut and wanted to apply his very considerable expertise in supplier-customer relationships in a more fact-based environment.

Jo's first action was to conduct a review of the global market for customer satisfaction research and of the major players in it, most of which were US-based. The brand leader at the time, or at least the company with the highest profile, was Walker Research, and Walker was wanting to license it's methodology world-wide. Active negotiations took place between Infratest Burke and Walker, but Walker was unwilling – quite understandably – to give the whole European franchise to one company, and Infratest Burke wasn't prepared to settle for anything less. So the negotiations foundered, which in retrospect was the best thing that could have happened!

Jo then decided to invent his own product, and I had the privilege of being asked to work with him on it. The idea was that Jo, as the 'Consultant', would provide the Customer Satisfaction expertise and I would ensure that his ideas were practical from a market research point of view – although in fact Jo was a much better market researcher and statistician than anybody gave him credit for. [There was a certain irony in all this. Jo, as a Consultant, couldn't possibly be a proper market researcher; whereas at the time all the market researchers in the company were claiming to be 'consultants'!]

Jo and I would meet once every 6-8 weeks in Munich to discuss where his ideas in terms of a CS product had got to. I wish I had kept some of the flip charts from those meetings, covered in Jo's scribblings, with boxes and triangles, inverted pyramids and Ven diagrams, all connected by arrows and in different colours that meant something. The trouble from my point of view was that each time we got together, Jo's ideas had moved on several steps from where we were the previous time: what we had previously thought was a promising avenue was apparently all wrong and now we were going off in a different direction! More than once during this period Hartmut Kiock, then CEO of Infratest Burke, would ask me what progress I thought we were making: "You see, Ian, Jo comes into my office and completely convinces me. Then 10 minutes later I can't remember a thing he's said!"

This went on for several months until at the beginning of our 5th or 6th meeting Jo turned a page of the flip chart over, and there was the Grid – and everything fell into place. My recall is that the concept for the Grid was almost complete and as it is now right from that point: the Index took a bit longer to refine and define.

4

1.3   The TRI*M Index

Most Customer Satisfaction surveys at the time included some variant or another of the first three TRI*M Index questions, namely Overall Satisfaction, Recommendation and Repurchase Intent. But in nearly all cases these three questions were treated as three different variables; or rather Overall Satisfaction would be treated as the key criterion variable, with Recommendation and Repurchase Intent being treated as useful secondary variables. Only very rarely was any attempt made to combine the responses to all three questions, one such case being Burke USA's 'Happy Customer Index', calculated as the percentage of customers giving the supplier a top-box rating on all three measures.

However, the '3 top box' approach not only is not an index in the true sense of the word, but a percentage, but it takes no account of the distribution of responses across the scales. That is, a supplier with a HCI of 35 might have 35% of its customers giving it a top-box rating on all three measures, with the other 65% giving it second-box ratings throughout , i.e. a very positive result. Equally it could mean that 35% give it top-box ratings and the other 65% give it bottom-box ratings – not likely, but a distinctly negative result that does not show up in the HCI measure.

That the TRI*M Index is a true index, reflecting all the scale responses and not just the top-box results, gives a more complete measure of customer loyalty (and, incidentally, is more stable since one or two percent of customers shifting from a top-box to a second-box rating on one of the questions will have virtually no impact on the TRI*M Index, whereas an HCI-type measure would go down one or two points).
The TRI*M Index was – and still is – virtually unique. It was also the tool that probably did most to get us away from thinking mainly about **satisfaction** and more about the quality of the whole customer-supplier relationship and **retention**. And we began to think that there was something missing from the 3-question Index.

If you think about it, satisfied customers who will recommend the product and buy it again are what the **supplier** wants from the relationship. Apart from preferring to be satisfied than not, there's very little in this from the customer's perspective.

The point emerged clearly in the automotive industry. It didn't seem right that BMW and Ford should have virtually identical TRI*M Indexes, but they did because BMW and Ford owners could be equally satisfied within

within the context of their expectations of their cars, equally likely to recommend them to friends in the market for the same level of car and equally likely to buy a BMW/Ford respectively the next time around. What was missing was the expectations fulfilment element, hence the Competitive Advantage question 'how big an advantage is it to you to have a BMW (Ford) rather than another make of car?'

The resulting four-question Index was not only more comprehensive, but more sensitive to market situations with different expectations levels (and with different fulfilment levels against those expectations).

1.4   The TRI*M Grid

Incorporating both Stated Importance and Calculated Importance in the TRI*M model and using them to define the axes of a familiar 4-quadrant Grid was a master stroke (as was using a form of correlation for the Calculated Importance dimension).

At the time there were two schools of thought as to how Importance should be defined:

- Gap Analysis, which in essence presented the results in terms of the difference between the performance rating for each quality item and it's stated importance rating. This was particularly prevalent in the USA.
- Regression, where importance was defined by the regression coefficients of each independant variable (quality elements, or more likely groups of quality elements) when regressed against a dependant variable such as Overall Satisfaction.

Incorporating both measures of Importance in the TRI*M model and using a form of correlation rather than regression were very brave and innovative things to do – although, as soon as Jo presented it, it was so obviously 'right'. Probably only a non-market researcher thinking outside the box could have come up with it!

At least in Europe, stated importance and correlation were thought at that time to be very old-fashioned.

Many studies had shown that calculated importance was different from stated importance; since calculated importance using trusted statistical techniques was obviously a 'better', more scientific measure, this meant that stated importance was unreliable or even wrong; so market researchers had for some years rejected stated importance as a measure and relied entirely on some form of calculated importance (it also saved on questionnaire space!).

What Jo realised was that, even if respondents' perceptions of what is important are at variance with what does in fact influence their attitudes/behaviour, the fact remains that this is what they **think** is important, and this cannot be ignored. Stated importance isn't wrong, it's just a different form of reality.

There are two main objections to correlation which regression theoretically overcomes. Firstly, correlation is a measure of association, not necessarily of causation; or at least, if there is causation, you don't know in which direction it is acting. And secondly, it takes no account of inter-correlation, or colinearity. However, in practice causation can be inferred, and inter-correlation is shown by the way quality items cluster on the Grid. Further, regression cannot really deal with anything more than 10-15 items at the most, so the only way of using it in the Customer Satisfaction context, where there might typically be 40-60 items, is to apply it at the category level (e.g. all product performance issues together, the sales process, after sales service, etc), which loses granularity and/or requires a two-step process – e.g. regressing the individual quality items within categories, and then regressing the categories against the overall criterion variable. Either way, you can't get it all on one chart!

Another master stroke was to decide to present everything on the Grid in relative rather than absolute terms. Apart from the fact that this fits in with the principle of continuous quality improvement and that what one wants to know anyway is what is relatively more/less important, or what is a relative strength / weakness, and not imagine that there is some absolute level of importance / performance to be aimed at, there was a very pragmatic reason for using relative data.

With absolute data, all the items could cluster in one area of the Grid which was evidently nonsensical in relation to the four Grid quadrants. Alternatively one could define the location of the 'cross,' and thus of the quadrants, in relation to the particular data set; but this would mean that the cross would be in different places on the Grid for different data sets, making it difficult to compare Grids from, say, one country to another, or from one time period to another. Using relative data solved this problem – and was consistent with the principles of quality and customer management.

1.5   The Impact of TRI*M

TRI*M has been a very successful product. It also contributed significantly to the integration of Infatest+Burke as a single company, and continues to do so now within TNS. TRI*M proved the point that product expertise is transferable, and the TRI*M network, backed up by the TRI*M Centre, is a model for any global product.

A lot has happened over the last 20 years since TRI*M first saw the light of day. The TRI*M methodology has been extended to apply to other stakeholder groups – to employees, to shareholders, to suppliers and so on – and not just to customers; and the application of TRI*M has been extended out of its B-to-B/capital goods heartland to consumer packaged goods markets too.

The methodology has also been continuously developed. The TRI*M Typology and the TRI*M Competitive Strengths and Weaknesses Analysis were early developments. More recently the TRI*M Bundles analysis has refined the way in which TRI*M can be used for detailed target setting; and the TRI*M Process and Execution Analysis (based on the Six Sigma concept) measures yet another aspect of customer satisfaction, namely the consistency of product and process performance as experienced by customers. Throughout all these changes and innovations, the TRI*M Index and the TRI*M Grid have remained the 'backbones' of the TRI*M methodology – there is virtually no TRI*M project that doesn't rely on the pioneering thoughts that Jo had some 20 years ago.

2 The Food Industry: Using TRI*M for Product Improvement

Pavel Holka

2.1 Introduction

Nestlé is the largest food producer in the world, with Nestlé Česko being the largest food producer in both the Czech Republic and Slovakia. There is a wide range of products available on the market, from ice-creams, confectionery, coffee, and cocoa to basic foodstuffs, infant foods, and pet foods.

For Nestlé, unlike the majority of FMCG giants, the coexistence of global and local brands are rather typical. Big global brands such as Nestlé Nescafé, Maggi, Kit Kat, and Purina live alongside big local brands such as Orion (a chocolate-confectionery umbrella brand) and Bon Pari (sweets). What they have in common is that all of them, with a few specific exceptions, are mainstream products aimed at frequent consumption among the majority of the population.

Nestlé operates two confectionery factories in the Czech Republic: one for sweets and one for chocolate. In Slovakia, Nestlé operates one factory, which produces foods such as soups and sauces. All three factories produce consumer products not only for the Czech and Slovak markets, but also for the whole region and even the whole of Europe. The aim is to produce high-quality products at reasonably competitive prices.

Nestle Cesko also imports some products from other countries, such as cocoa from Hungary and wafers from Poland. This implies that it is necessary to deal with each product differently in terms of recipe development.

It is only logical that products available only on the Czech and Slovak markets are adapted to the tastes of Czech and Slovak consumers. Despite the fact that it is not easy to find average recipes for one or two similar markets, it is nonetheless easier than finding average recipes for five, six, or even ten or more, markets. Luckily, there is a system of product testing for the whole of the Nestlé world with the same principle, rules, and method, which allows us to compare the results among all of the countries involved. This system is known as 60/40.

2.2   What Is 60/40?

The term 60/40 has become a buzzword that everyone who is working for Nestlé and with Nestlé products (marketing people, research-and-development people, and quality-audit people) understands, no matter whether he or she is from the Czech Republic or, for example, Malaysia. The main objective of Nestlé's 60/40 (60/40+ since 2005) business tool is to achieve taste and nutritional superiority over competitors' products in order to communicate the specifics of this superiority to consumers. The name of this tool comes from the desired result of a product-preference test. Two products are compared: one Nestle and one from a competitor. The desired result is that at least 60% of consumers prefer the Nestlé product to the competitor product, hence 60/40. This tool is not used separately, of course; it is used as an integral part of a knowledge base.

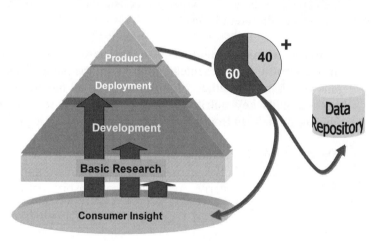

Fig. 1. The Success of 60/40+ Depends on the Usage of Common Knowledge Gained from a Data Repository, Consumer Insights, Research & Development, and Technology

The 60/40+ process is continuous and has four main pillars:

1. **Consumer (Taste) Preference Test:** This is a sequential monadic test with paired comparison. All products are tested blind (if practicable) in order to eliminate the influence of branding, packaging, and product concept as much as possible. This is the part with the greatest weight in the whole process.

2. **Sensory Profile:** Each product is sensorially tested by a panel of trained taste testers. The results of this part provide answers regarding which attributes are weaker and which are stronger for the Nestlé product in comparison with the competitor product—for example, whether or not the Nestle product is sweeter than the competitor product—but without determining whether it is perceived as better or worse by consumers. (This is the task of Consumer Preference Test.)

3. **Nutritional Assessment:** This is the newest part of the whole process and it is represented by the '+' in the name. This provides answers as to whether or not the product meets expectations regarding its key nutritional factors, based on legal regulations, dietary guidelines from health authorities, and Nestlé policies.

4. **Product Improvement:** This part gives the whole process continuity and involves a cross-functional team comprising people from marketing, market research, the sensory network, R&D, technology, etc.

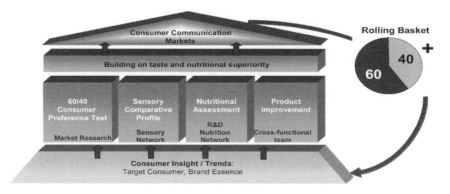

Fig. 2. The 60/40+ Process Is Continuous and Incorporates Different Company Functions

2.3   The Incorporation of TRI*M into 60/40+

The question is, why do we use TRI*M when we have such a great tool for product development? The answer is simple. From time to time—and as time has passed, it has happened more and more frequently—a case arises when a simple comparison of two products based on monadic values has not been sufficient. In quite a large proportion of tests, preferences were 50/50, without any clear hints or clues as to how the respective products could be improved. Because 60/40 is an important KPI of top and middle management, this issue had to be resolved.

We implemented TRI*M, in co-operation with TNS AISA, at the beginning of 2005. TNS AISA exclusively conducts all 60/40 consumer-preference tests and the majority of product tests for Nestlé. As 60/40 only focuses on one 'P' from the marketing mix, which is 'Product', we only use 'Product TRI*M' for this purpose. The hardest aspect of this was to incorporate TRI*M questions into the preference-test questionnaire in such a way that the standard interview flow could be maintained. Because the questionnaire is quite standardized for the whole of the Nestlé world, apart from some specifics for different product categories and local needs, we had quite limited latitude in terms of questionnaire modification.

As we only did this locally, for the Czech and Slovak market, we used a false-trial approach. Finally, some time in June 2005, we settled upon the final version of the master questionnaire. Since then, TRI*M has been used for all 60/40+ product tests and the majority of concept and product tests. This has resulted in the creation of a huge database of TRI*M indices containing over 100 products and concepts. TRI*M is on the way to becoming a standard KPI, next to 60/40, market share, and EBITA. However, this is not yet truly the case.

2.4   An Example of TRI*M Usage in Product Development

This example shows how we use TRI*M for product development:

In this particular case, we obtain no clear preference score based on the standard 60/40 evaluation; we lacked two different attributes. The TRI*M indices for the Nestlé product (71) and the competitor product (69) were high. The TRI*M grid provided us with three attributes on which, among others, we had focused during the process of product development, although these three attributes were not identified in the monadic evaluation table as disadvantages in the face of the competition.

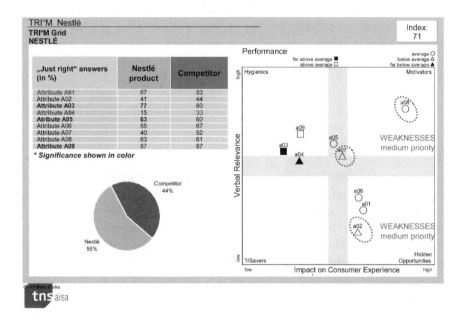

Fig. 3a. Test #1. This Shows the Monadic Evaluations of Several Attributes, Preferences, and the TRI*M Grid

Based on results from TRI*M analysis, we focused on these three attributes, which were identified as being of medium weakness. After a few months of recipe development and laboratory testing, an improved formula was ready for 60/40 product testing. We also incorporated more attributes into the questionnaire, which proved difficult to cover during recipe development.

This whole process resulted in the improvement of our TRI*M index from 71 to 78 and clear 60/40 preference. In the short term, we decided to keep the original recipe, as it was superior to that of the competitor product and the index was marginally higher. In the mid term, the focus was to be on other relative weaknesses, which were revealed in the second test.

14

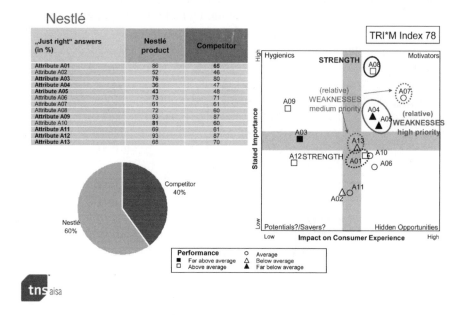

Fig. 3b. Test #2: This Shows the Monadic Evaluations of Several Attributes, Preference, and the TRI*M Grid

2.5 Next Steps

TRI*M is used not only in 60/40, but also on an ad-hoc basis. TRI*M has become an integral part of all local product and concept testing. With the implementation of SAP and pressure on one-number reporting, the TRI*M index is likely to increase its importance.

In July 2007, TRI*M was incorporated into the continuous Nestlé Brand Health Tracker, and it is now used to monitor brand and product performance. When a TRI*M index falls significantly, the Consumer TRI*M Module is applied.

3 How Can Market Research Findings Lead to Lasting Improvements Within a Company?

Gudrun Kneißl

3.1 Starting Point: Customer Surveys Are Now Used Universally, but They Do Not Result Automatically in a Smooth Implementation Process

Virtually every company now measures and monitors customer satisfaction and customer retention. However, it does not necessarily mean that this will lead to an implementation process and specific measures being introduced once the results have been presented. Whilst it is generally agreed that there is a need for improvements to be made, this often remains a good intention. This raises the question: why, when enthusiasm and the reliability of the results encourage action to be taken, does this remain an intention? The lack of a process manager is a major factor which prevents intentions from being translated into actions. Since there are plenty of potential courses of action, a company must decide on one and pursue it consistently. Which method will be suitable for the company depends on parameters such as capacities and the organisational structure as well as the improvement processes already in place at the company.

The most important jobs of the process manager are therefore:

- To verify the parameters
- To define the implementation process
- To check the processes in place for overlapping areas and/or ability to integrate with the implementation process
- To establish cornerstones
- To coordinate the meeting of deadlines and performance of tasks
- To monitor compliance with them

What might sound simple at first will, however, require consistent, long-term effort coupled with a great deal of intuition. It is a job that demands a lot of time.

3.2 How Can this Sort of Implementation Process Be Set Up in Practice?

For an implementation process to succeed, an eye should always be kept on the whole project. And, with this knowledge, favourable conditions for implementing the results should be put in place when the project is set up.

3.2.1 Favourable Conditions for an Efficient Implementation Process

It is helpful if, ahead of the market research project, consideration is given to what the company hopes to achieve with the results. On the one hand, to ensure that all the necessary components have been integrated into the study, and on the other, to facilitate acceptance of the results more easily. This means agreeing the specific objective of the project beforehand to enable a purpose-built programme to be developed. Everyone who may later be affected in any way by the results should be involved in formulating the objectives. These people should be deciding on the specifics of the programme to ensure that all points of view and requirements which may have an impact on future measures are included.

Furthermore, for the purposes of subsequent analysis and interpretations of results, a decision must be made on which customer groups, market segments, regions, product groups, etc. need to be capable of being analysed separately to allow group-typical details to be extracted from the information collected.

The selection of an established market research institute will help considerably in improving confidence in the results generated and will also help to provide benchmark data through which a company can analyse its own results meaningfully. At the same time, the institute's experience will guarantee that all essential building blocks are included.

TNS Infratest with their TRI*M method for measuring customer retention meets all of the important preconditions set out above:

- TNS Infratest is an established market research institute which meets the highest qualitative standards – applied uniformly worldwide.

- TRI*M has been used in many branches of industry and several thousand studies and is consequently both tried and tested and has been built on. And, on the other, it is able to supply benchmark data, including sector-specific data.

- With the methods it employs, the institute supplies results that show at a glance a company's lever (i.e. its significance and influence in the marketplace) and how it should prioritise in this context.

3.2.2 Introducing the Implementation Process

At the beginning of the process there is both organisational and analytical work to be done to ensure successful implementation.

Organising Implemenation

Since the sections of the company which are to benefit from the customer survey will have been defined before the survey is started, a date for a joint workshop should be agreed with the section heads, regional heads and the management. The date for the workshop must be scheduled to take place soon after the date set for the presentation of the results so that it does not take too long before the actual implementation can start and yet there is sufficient time left for the results to be processed to decide which topics will be discussed at the workshop.

The cornerstones that need to be reached during the implementation process following the management workshop to monitor the process should be specified in a schedule.

All these organisational tasks should be performed by the process manager who should be defined and identified in advance as process supervisor. The process manager will define the procedure – i.e. the implementation process itself – and specify the schedule. The process manager should have the necessary capacities at his disposal to supervise the process.

Analyses Which Simplify the Generation of Actions to Be Taken

When the survey data is available, analyses which show which performance elements are genuine drivers for customer retention and purchase decisions will help to identify control levers. These drivers must also be considered in the context of all performance elements surveyed in order to identify links and interaction.

For example, the following findings were made when this all-embracing analysis was used in a sample company: In the eyes of customers, the "good will" performance element was very important and also had a very strong impact on customer retention and, moreover, scored surprisingly highly. Generally speaking, "good will" will only have a very high status if the customers have to make use of good will and if this is the case product defects and/or quality problems are often responsible for this. However, product quality was excellent at the sample company and could not, therefore, have been responsible for the high customer retention effect of good will. Since the results also showed that although customers were price-sensitive, they nonetheless rated the price-performance ratio of the products highly, the conclusion to be drawn from the sum of these results was that they may be concealing hidden discounts. A discussion with sales staff confirmed this: Instead of being given direct discounts, the customer was promised upgrades once the machine had been installed which was then declared to be good will. This discovery led to the price and conditions policy being included as a topic in the implementation process.

Cross-analysis and identification of the real drivers provide information on a company's weaknesses or strengths and how these affect customers. In a first step, negative and positive retention drivers can be created from this and prioritised. As well as prioritising in accordance with the driver strengths, 'quick wins' should also be identified, i.e. the performance elements which can be used to achieve a positive effect quickly and cost-effectively. This way, customers will be quick to identify changes, the company's credibility will be increased and there will be a positive impact on the readiness of customers to participate in subsequent surveys.

Implementation Process

Scenarios can be created using the relevant strengths and weaknesses, considering quick wins, which can then be discussed by the decision-makers. The preparatory analytical work should help, above all, managers to use the little time at their disposal efficiently. That means that the analyses will not take place jointly within this circle, rather, the most important results will already have been processed earlier, which means that the decision-makers need only prioritise the elements upon which the implementation process will be based.

Firstly, the process will run top-down. Management stipulates the topic areas which are tackled on the basis of analyses and in line with the company's strategic goals. Members of staff will be assigned to each topic area and they will be responsible for dealing with it and, if necessary, putting together a team or seeking support elsewhere, e.g. in the case of regional themes, in the region. From this point onwards the process becomes a bottom-up process because the teams have no authority to make decisions and the superiors must sanction implementation of the measure.

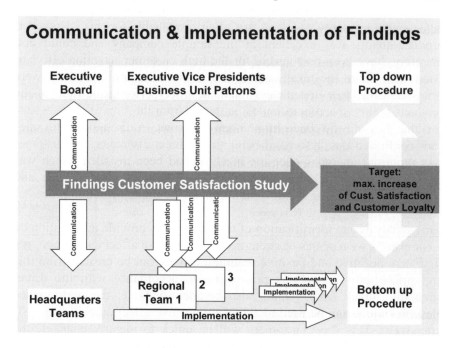

Fig. 1. Communication & Implementation of Findings

Management Workshop to Establish the Areas of Action and Teams

The best way to begin the implementation process once the results of a customer retention study have been presented is to hold a management workshop. The process manager – who will often act simultaneously as the facilitator, will prepare the scenarios. It is recommended that these scenarios are verified with the institute that carried out the analyses and with the appropriate internal specialist departments to preclude misinterpretations.

The format set out below can be used to prepare for the workshop:

- Explanation: What are the areas of action?
- What were the reasons for the performance evaluation of the drivers?
- Clarification of how to link performance elements to potential areas of action.

This list of potential areas of action should now be discussed and decisions taken on the following:

- o **Areas of action,** their link to performance elements and their global/local significance
- o **Priority** of the areas of action: 1, 2 or 3 (priority-1 areas of action should be dealt with first)
- o **Implementation teams** for priority-1 areas of action should be created.
  Implementation team list

Area of action (Description)	Team members	Team leader	Monitoring/ Controlling ("Patron")	Reporting channel /deadlines	Implementation deadlines
….	…	….	…	…	….

Establishing Action Fields

Examples of working scenarios to be used to establish action fields are illustrated below. Something they all have in common is that the topics tackled are highly relevant to customer retention and are therefore all potential areas of action.

Examples of working scenarios to generate measures:

Scenario 1:

Good will is extremely important to customers from a particular sphere of business and is rated highly particularly in some regions (despite high satisfaction with the reliability of machines). Are hidden discounts concealed behind this?

Scenario 2:

The follow-up visiting rate of sales partners – in particular after a sale has been concluded – is insufficient for our customers.
How can better customer care be provided?

Scenario 3:

Contactability and response time in cases of failure are not good enough and mainly poorer than that of competitors.
What are competitors doing better?

Scenario 4:

Availability of spare parts is a problem (apart from in northern Europe).
Why is that?

Scenario 5:

Customs would like more information on new lines as well as on the company's strategy and alignment.
Why do our customers feel they do not receive sufficient information?

Scenario 6:

The energy consumption of the machines is criticised and that of competitors judged to be better. Objective testing shows, however, that the machines are the most economical in comparison with competitors.
How can we convince customers of comparatively low energy consumption?

Since limited resources generally mean that not all action fields can be dealt with, the management's most important job is to prioritise potential tasks. This may mean a brief discussion of the scenarios offered to make sure that

- the process manager's interpretation is shared,
- there is a common understanding of the area of action,
- the person(s) responsible for dealing with an issue can be identified.

Questions arising from these scenarios are a good way of generating discussion.

Process of the Implementation of Findings

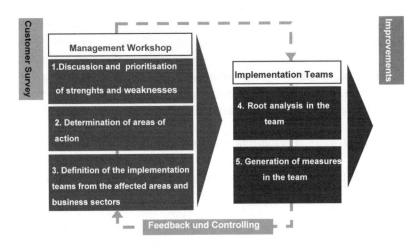

Fig. 2. Process of the Implementation of Findings

Prioritising the Areas of Action

If so many of the scenarios selected remain in the relevant set of possible areas of action that they cannot all be processed (which is usually the case), they will have to be prioritised by, for example, awarding points in accordance with the following questions:

Green points: "What can we tackle first/is it achievable?"
= chance of solution, quick wins

Red points: What should we tackle first?"
= pressure to act

Additionally, feedback relating to ongoing processes will be required before prioritisation can take place:

- o Check which ongoing projects/processes could benefit from partial results from the market research study
- o Incorporate the customer survey findings into ongoing projects
- o Check whether other projects/processes have already started relevant measures which could be linked – e.g. balanced scorecard processes
- o Exploit the synergy effect
- o Avoid duplication

A patron who can assume responsibility at a functional level and for matters requiring approval should be assigned for the topics prioritised on the basis of the abovementioned points (e.g. by attaching points). He will have the authority to decide whether and by whom specific courses of action should be taken. The next thing to do is to consider how these courses of action should be worked out.

Find "Worker Bees" to Work out the Actions

So, who should take care of the specific to-do list? Answering this question is the next task of managers during the workshop.

What are actions? Specific to-do items could be actions to improve a situation. However, they could also be analytical tasks which must be undertaken first so that the problem can be illustrated more clearly. If, for example, the handling of complaints has been criticised, the following questions can be analysed:

- o Is there a complaint management process and are there any shortcomings in the process?
- o Are there shortcomings in respect of the person receiving the complaint or problems with how complaints are dealt with?
- o What are the complaints? Could systemic problems or quality shortfalls lie behind them?

The following rule generally applies: the type of action field involved should be borne in mind when selecting the "worker bees". This may be an individual or a team.

The following guidelines should be adhered when deciding on the composition of the team:

o   The team members must have the necessary specialist skills
o   Members must be team-players and be capable of working together constructively
o   Realistic participation in team activities must be possible (time, location)
o   Members should come from not just one sector but, as far as possible, from all sectors affected by the topic or which could provide valuable input (not stew in their own juice)
o   The teams should not be too big (maximum of 6 people)
o   And last but not least, members should work together voluntarily and happily

For managers this means that they can only make suggestions on how the team should be composed and must obtain the consent of the persons concerned for this. It is the job of the process manager or patron to recruit the right team members to collaborate in the implementation process.

General Objectives and Guidelines for Processing the Areas of Action

Now that the areas of action have been defined and the associated action teams established, important cornerstones within the implementation process need to be considered. The process manager will supervise and organise them.

1.   What is the intended overall objective of the implementation process?

     Recommendation: Set out in writing e.g.: Ensure optimum fulfilment of important customer requirements which represent a key buying factor in the basic model. Increase customer retention and profitability of certain customer groups to value X, etc.

2.   What is the latest date for teams to be formed?

     Recommendation: As soon as possible, no later than after 4 weeks.

3.   How will work be monitored? What are the reporting channels? What are the reporting times and forms?

     Recommendation: Reporting times, channels and forms should be stipulated. A joint reporting meeting is an advantage when several teams are working on areas of action at the same time.

This should take place every 3 - 4 months in the presence of the patrons and team leaders. The team results and the team leaders' suggested courses of action will be presented at these meetings, during which any overlapping areas can be identified and eliminated. The patrons will then decide jointly or the team leader alone which actions should be undertaken and by whom. The teams will then implement the actions. A single sheet of actions should be completed for the records.

4. What time frame should be kept to for the overall process?

    Recommendation: A manageable time frame which at the same time allows a realistic time for the course of action to be taken, taking into account the time required for it and the ease with which it can be implemented. A period of 1 - 2 years often proves reasonable for a process.

Following the implementation process, the follow-up study for monitoring actions undertaken will be included in plans.

Now, the teams can be put together and the processing can begin. Don't forget though:

The management is responsible for implementing the measures generated!

3.2.3   Processing the Areas of Action

First of all, a clear illustration of the established areas of action and areas of responsibility for which the team has assumed responsibility should be presented. The procedure illustrated in Fig. 3 is often used to great effect for the specific processing of the area of action by the persons responsible or the team.

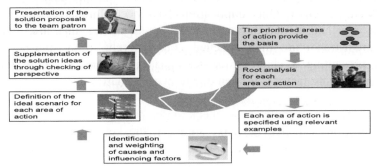

Fig. 3. Cause Analysis and Collection of Solution Proposals

Crystallising Case Studies and Finding Solution Ideas:

Each working group can write the area of action on a Metaplan chart and attach it to the middle of the pin-board. Questions such as "What does the customer mean or "How did this customer perception come about?" can also help to interpret the results of a market research study.

Typical case studies show that:
To crystallise the area of action it helps to find as many causes as possible: e.g. in the case of poor communication: What type of communication? Are the channels or media poor? When and under what conditions is it poor?

Please Note: It Does Not Help to Identify the Guilty Party!

The following methods can be used to collect influencing factors and/or causes:

o   Brainwriting:
    Each group member is given a sheet of paper to write down in three minutes what he or she thinks are the key influencing factors of a particular area of action. The sheet is then passed on to the person sitting next to him or her and each person is given one minute to supplement the notes made so far. The sheet is passed on until each person is once more holding his or her original sheet. The contents of the sheets are then collected and identified causes (once any duplication has been eliminated) are written down on Metaplan charts.

- o Metaplan technique:
  Each group member writes down an influencing factor on a Metaplan chart. Once duplications have been eliminated, the chart is attached to a pin-board. Influencing factors that are more downstream are then attached consecutively to the pin-board, representing a chain of causes. It is important that only one influencing factor is written down on each chart.

Consolidate causes (completeness, check of perspective):
Further questions can help to make sure that the key causes have been recorded. This may include, for example:

"Will our problem be solved if we eliminate all this?"
"Have we recorded all the causes?"
Check of perspective:
"What would your colleagues say?"
"How do customers or suppliers see it?"
"What would management say?"

Any new or downstream causes identified should be added to the list of causes. The causes should then be evaluated so that priorities can be set on the basis of this evaluation. Clearly identified causes will act as a template for solution-finding since specific to-do items can often be easily identified as a result.

Methods for collecting ideas:

- Calling-out
- Brainstorming based on the following rules:

  - o Quantity instead of quality
  - o Each suggestion is important because it will lead to new associations
  - o The only limitation: Only solutions which a person can influence himself
  - o Realistic solutions are then selected
  - o Quantity instead of quality
  - o Each suggestion is important because it will lead to new associations
  - o The only limitation: Only solutions which a person can influence himself
  - o Realistic solutions are then selected

Feedback Loops and Documentation

The solution ideas generated now need to be agreed with the patron or the relevant person in charge. The identification and discussion of measures that will help to improve the drivers should stand in the foreground. A decision now needs to be made as whether an action will result from these measures and who will be responsible for implementing it. The measures therefore enter the following feedback loop:

- o The team leader reports the working group's results to the patron or at the reporting meeting (bottom-up)
- o Feedback from patrons to Team (top-down)
- o Supplementation of the proposed solutions/measures generated, if required
- o Report suggested solutions to management
- o Once agreement has been reached, the measures are implemented by the team, with the support of the patron

The documenting of the progress of a team's work is another important point:
All the points relevant to an area of action are recorded on a sheet detailing the measures to be taken:

- o Description of the area of action
- o Description of the measure
- o Specific actions
- o Who is responsible for this?
- o How long will it take to implement the measures
- o How much work has already been done (percentage)

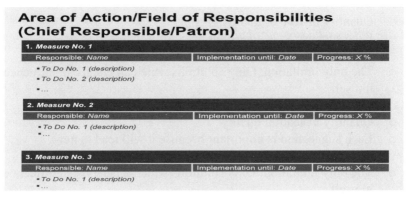

Fig. 4. Presentation Template for Documenting Implementation of Measures

It is the process manager's job to organise all the abovementioned feedback and reporting loops. The collection of status reports from the teams handling the measures is a key part of organisation. It is recommended that forms such as those given as examples in the figures are used for this. This will enable an overview of all measures and the stage they are at to be prepared without difficulty.

3.3   Conclusion

The effectiveness of a process for implementing measures depends on how well the following points are dealt with:

o   The definition and organisation of the implementation process
o   The availability of a process manager to supervise, monitor and organise the entire process
o   The importance attached by management to this process

So, if a well-conceived and organised process is in place, management is fully behind this process and failure will attract consequences, the chances of a successful implementation are virtually 100%.

Finally, providing customers with feedback can also produce positive results. For example, a customer could be thanked for taking part in the survey by email or letter. If a customer is told of some of the measures developed, he or she will see involvement in a survey of this type as a valuable use of his or her time and adopt a positive attitude towards future surveys.

Based on the example of an internationally-active German mechanical-engineering company's use of the results of a customer-retention survey.
Dedicated to Dr. Joachim Scharioth, someone I found to be an excellent teacher and who always selflessly shared his extensive knowledge.

4   The TRI*M Principle-Applying It in the Public Sector

Eric Sondervan

TRI*M is one of the leading systems in the area of Stakeholder Management. TRI*M was originally designed for the profit sector. Since more than a decade, some twelve thousand studies have taken place for a great many companies, from small and medium-sized businesses to the blue-chips of this world. More than half of the Fortune 100 companies use (or have used) TRI*M.

TRI*M has a long track record in the profit sector, with its use widely spread over various regions, industry sectors and company sizes. There is hardly any difference in the way the TRI*M tools are applied to the different industry sectors. The four TRI*M Index Questions fit perfectly, whether it is a company from the financial sector, the energy sector, the retail sector, or the IT sector. There is also a special Consumer TRI*M for FMCG companies. As the client relations are different in this sector, not the supplier/manufacturer is the subject of research, but the product.

4.1   Applying TRI*M in the Public Sector

Enough said about TRI*M in the profit sector. The non-profit sector is more diverse. Public authorities/institutions differ widely in their structures and roles. Most public authorities (such as register offices) work in a non-competitive environment and thus the users of their services have no choice, whereas other public authorities operate in a competitive environment which closely resembles the situation of any company in a market environment. For example, kindergartens are often in a competitive situation because parents are able to choose between private and public kindergartens. The latter public institutions should be approached with a regular TRI*M Customer Retention study, taking into account the competitive situation and freedom of choice available to the recipient of the service. Genuine public institutions such as municipalities, schools, hospitals, nursing homes and central/national governments all have their similarities when it comes to applying the TRI*M principle. The measuring dimensions can, however, be different.

'Recommendation', 'repeat purchase' and 'competitive advantage' (all of which are TRI*M Index Questions) have no meaning, or at least a different meaning, in the non-profit sector compared to the profit sector. 'Trust' and 'value to society' are more applicable. Nowadays the situation is even more complicated because in various countries there is an ongoing trend towards privatisation in some (former) public sectors such as the energy sector or the post sector. As a result people can choose from and compare various providers. This creates a new situation in which the discussion is whether the TRI*M Index Questions for the profit sector or the TRI*M Index Questions for the non-profit sector are applicable.

Competitive situation	Non-competitive situation
1. Overall performance	1. Overall performance
2. Recommendation	2. Trust
3. Repurchase	3. Value to society
4. Competitive advantage	4. Comparison

Fig. 1. TRI*M Index Questions in Two Market Situations

4.2 The Added Value of the TRI*M Tools in the Public Sector

As the grey area between the public and private sector is so diverse, one has to be cautious in applying the appropriate TRI*M Index Questions. When 'competitive advantage' is not applicable and 'comparison' is used, one has to be careful what to compare it with. Take the National Association of Dentists. One might say a comparison with other associations would be right. But does a dentist have experience with other, comparable associations? We would not want to compare it with the association of philatelists, would we? Or with the blood bank, an institution for collecting blood in order to redistribute it to those who need it most urgently. Should we compare their service quality with a general practitioner's or a hospital's service quality?

The experience concept might also have a different meaning. Public institutions are often established to fulfill a certain public task which is important to society, an institution for national security, for instance.

There is no direct customer relation to an average citizen, but still this citizen experiences its services, albeit in a passive way. There are many public institutions which only a limited number of people have recent experiences with. In order to measure service quality in this situation, a sample of recent users must be delivered the principle of the research.

In the public sector reputation (or image) is also very important. Public institutions are established with the objective to serve the public in a certain way. The barriers for people to make use of the institution should be as limited as possible. When people have little or no experience, the image of the institution is important. When trying to improve the service quality, an institution can experience resistance due to a negative image. A tax office having difficulties to implement new tax rules resulting in negative press/media coverage will first have to regain trust before a quality measure will have sufficient effect. We can use TRI*M Corporate Reputation to measure an institution's image.

TRI*M Corporate Reputation manager is based on five questions:

- Overall reputation
- Favorability
- Trust
- Success
- Product and service quality

Here too, a little creativity is sometimes necessary; 'success' can have different meanings for a hospital and a tax office. Every institution delivers something, but 'products and services' is not an unambiguous concept for, for instance, a nursing home; people may interpret it differently. Therefore the TRI*M Index Questions should be made-to-measure on some occasions, e.g. by changing a few words in the original question and/or by adding a few examples.

		Objective of the project	
		Measurement of satisfaction/ retention of external clients/users	Measurement of reputation (target groups: general Public...)
Type of organisation	Sovereign/ monopolistic public authorities	TRI*M Public Service Quality	TRI*M Corporate Reputation Manager
	Public authorities in competitive environment	TRI*M Customer Retention	TRI*M Corporate Reputation Manager
	Monopolistic companies in market environment	TRI*M Customer Retention with adapted questions*	TRI*M Corporate Reputation Manager

Fig. 2. Organisation Matrix

The TRI*M Typology in the public sector also has a different meaning. In the private sector we can, for instance, identify mercenaries, customers who are satisfied but who nevertheless switch to another supplier easily. Or we can identify hostages who are very loyal but not very satisfied. These hostages are often customers who cannot switch due to a lack of alternatives or a long-term contract with their supplier. When we project this on the public sector, we cannot use the concept of mercenaries, because most often there are no alternatives. The loyalty concept dimension of TRI*M as used in the private sector cannot be used as such in the public sector. However, the satisfaction concept can: it is the evaluation of the services of those who experienced them. A relevant dimension here is 'endorsement", which is all about the support an institution is expected to get when offering its services. The endorsement dimension is based on the two TRI*M Index Questions 'value to society' and 'comparison'. The score on this dimension is lower when an institution is offering services which are not contributing to the objectives for which the institution was established in the first place. This can be based on perception, which menas a different response not changing the offer, but improving the communication on the public services offered.

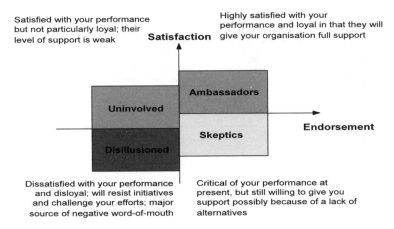

Fig. 3. Typology Public Sector

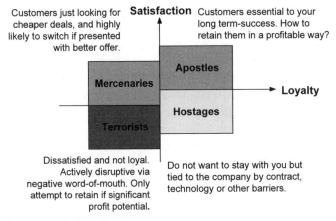

Fig. 4. Typology Private Sector

The TRI*M Grid also appears to be a very valuable diagnostic tool for the public sector in order to analyse what causes a high or low TRI*M Index. It does not only identify the key drivers of service quality, but also the Hygienics: not to fall below a specific quality level, which is a basic requirement for service orientation. And the hidden opportunities: these items give the potential to increase the institution's service orientation. This extra information makes the TRI*M Grid a unique diagnostic tool, better than a genuine driver analysis with only performance and (implicitly measured) importance.

36

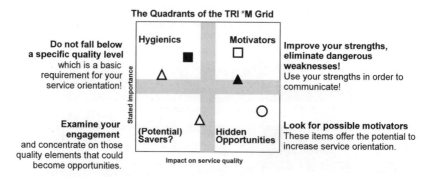

Fig. 5. Grid Explanation

The Global TRI*M Centre, as a centre of excellence in Stakeholder Management, has had considerable experience dealing with the abovementioned kind of situations during its long history. Times are changing, situations are changing, but the TRI*M principle has always been applicable.

The public sector particularly needs a certain amount of customisation, but the TRI*M diagnostics always give extra interesting insights. Some recent examples of Dutch practice will illustrate this:

The Global TRI*M Centre, as a centre of excellence in Stakeholder Management, has had considerable experience dealing with the abovementioned kind of situations during its long history. Times are changing, situations are changing, but the TRI*M principle has always been applicable.
The public sector particularly needs a certain amount of customisation, but the TRI*M diagnostics always give extra interesting insights. Some recent examples of Dutch practice will illustrate this:

Case 1: Evaluation of Measures Within Policy Areas Among the General Public

In the Netherlands, like in many other countries, there is a jungle of governmental rules and measures where the need to cut out at least the dead wood has become urgent nowadays. Government and citizens have reached a general agreement on this matter. But what are the underlying dimensions of how this burden of rules and measures are perceived?

How does the general public experience all the measures that were taken? Does the public experience these measures as clear, fair, costly, efficient, effective etc.?

A survey was carried out to answer these questions, and Dutch citizens were asked for their opinion. In the first phase, the exploratory phase, the evaluation was done on a more aggregated level. It seemed inappropriate to evaluate on the level of a single measure. In every policy area there is a jungle of bigger and smaller measures. Now how was the TRI*M principle applied?

Every citizen has a perception, an image of the governmental performance in a certain policy area. Experiences with measures within this policy area differ greatly. Therefore we decided to use TRI*M Corporate Reputation as the general framework and 20 policy areas were taken into consideration. There were some about which the majority of the citizens get no information through the media. They are not aware of anything that is going on in these policy areas.

The TRI*M Corporate Reputation Index can tell what the government's overall performance image is in a certain policy area: the TRI*M Index is the central indicator. The following dimensions were used:

- Perception of/experience with quality of measures
- Achieved results so far
- Reputation in that area (the past)
- Current overall impression (the present)
- Trust (the future)

Qualitative research preceding the quantitative measurement showed that the average citizen had limited knowledge of and experience with an individual measure. Nevertheless, the respondents were screened on awareness and minimum knowledge, to ensure that they had a clear opinion about the measures taken in a certain policy area on dimensions such as fair, clear, effective, costly etc.

The overall TRI*M Index resulting from the quantitative study was fairly low, which did not come unexpectedly because there were already experiences that (national) government in general gets much lower ratings than, for instance, suppliers of services in the private sector. We also know from experience that political parties get negative TRI*M Corporate Reputation Indices. The outcome of a global TRI*M survey (2005) was that the TRI*M Corporate Reputation score for the Netherlands was -18 (global TRI*M score for political parties was -10). Normally, in an 'average' TRI*M survey for the private sector, the top-2 box score is much higher than the bottom-2 box score. In this survey for the public sector it was the other way around.

	Bottom-2 box (%)
Perception of/experience with quality of measures	66
Achieved results so far	69
Reputation in that area (the past)	70
Current overall impression (the present)	46
Trust (the future)	32

It is remarkable that the citizens are relatively (!) optimistic when it comes to their trust in the future (in comparison to the other questions). The question here is what the right benchmark is. Will the general population ever give high ratings in the top-2 boxes of the TRI*M scale? How big are the differences between the various sub-sectors: national government, local government, semi-public institutions?

Once more, the TRI*M Typology appears to be of high value. When looking at the five TRI*M Questions we can identify two major dimensions:

- Perceived performance (quality of measures, achieved results in the recent past)
- Public support (reputation, impression, trust)

It can identify which part of the population:

- perceives a good (current) performance, but is not expected to give much support based on past experiences and future expectations;
- does not perceive a good (current) performance, but is supportive based on past experiences and future expectations;
- does not perceive a good (current) performance and is not expected to give much support. For most policy areas this is the biggest part.

The relative size of each of the four segments of the typology has a direct influence on the communication strategy. When a new measure is being implemented, having tailwind makes it much easier to get the desired effect than having headwind.

It appeared that the 'public support' dimension discriminated very well between the policy areas, varying from 72% to 18%. The first policy area is the environmental tax for brown and white goods, a well-accepted tax in the Netherlands; the second is the property tax, the value estimation of residences, on which a special tax is based. To approach the real value of the residence, the growth rate of this value estimation of real estate was rather high during the last few years. The reason for this was that it had started very low, not having a strong relation to the real value of the property. The consequence was that the tax also grew fast, which explains the low support.

The TRI*M Grid was the third TRI*M deliverable used in this study. It answers the question: which characteristics mostly affect the overall image of the policy area. The TRIM Grid gives insight into the strengths and weaknesses of policies/measures with respect to their content and communication.

40

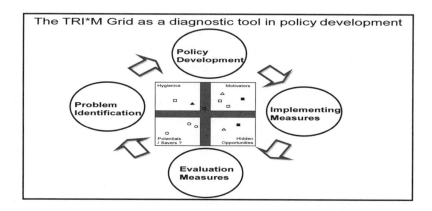

Fig. 6. The TRI*M Grid as a Diagnostic Tool in Policy Development

Besides answering the question 'what drives the overall appreciation of government policy in a certain area the most?', it answers many more questions. For instance, which characteristics are Hygienics, are 'musts' when it comes to developing individual measures? Or which characteristics are opportunities to improve the image if, for instance, more effort were put into communication?

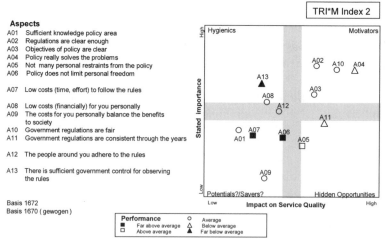

Fig. 7. Example of Grid

A common denominator is the aspect 'the measure really solves the problem', which was rated very low, considered to be very important and had a strong impact on the TRI*M Index. Based on past experiences, citizens clearly do not have much confidence that measures taken by the government will have any effect. Furthermore, measures taken are not always very consistent. Opinions about clearness and fairness are more divided but definitely a point of attention. Enforcing the rules is the area showing the greatest dissatisfaction. It is an aspect with little impact on the TRI*M Index, but which is considered as relatively important by the citizens. This aspect should therefore not be neglected. Limitation of freedom, effort, extra expenses, and burden are all (relatively) positively evaluated. These are all aspects that have a limited impact on the overall TRI*M Index.

Another valuable TRI*M tool appeared to be the so called P&E analysis based on the Six Sigma paradigm (strategic theory based measuring the variance of processes). It is very valuable to know whether it is a consistently low score when a certain policy area or specific measure scores badly on a certain dimension. There are two situations: the first one is that everybody criticises the government in their policymaking. The conclusion might be that either the content or the communication should be re-engineered. The second situation is that the overall scores are low but that there is a great variation. This variation could be caused by the fact that different target groups greatly differ in their opinions. This could mean that policies may need only minor adjustments; communication could help to improve the image among certain groups of people. The variation could also be caused by different measures within a policy area eliciting different reactions from people.

If the total of all policy areas is taken into consideration, we see that the aspects with a low score also have a lower variance than the aspects with a higher score. This means that there is a general agreement among the Dutch population that the government is performing badly on negatively rated aspects such as 'sufficient government control', 'policy really solves the problem' and 'policies are 'fair' The variation of the ratings is much higher on the positively rated aspects, meaning less agreement among the population. The most positively rated aspects are about personal restraints, as was shown above.

Case 2: A Syndicated Survey for Municipalities

The TRI*M principle has also proved its value to municipalities; the question here is which TRI*M tools to apply. Does an average citizen really experience everything a municipality is offering? Getting a new passport at the counter of the town hall is definitely an experience, but walking through the park, is that also an experience? Experiencing few obstacles when trying to have your say in local policies, is that also a real experience with tangible dimensions to measure?

We decided to use TRI*M to measure the total experience in the abovementioned syndicated survey. The TRI*M Questions for the public sector were applied:

- Overall performance: a citizen can give an overall judgment, at least has an opinion about the municipality where they reside.
- Trust: influences retention; when there is no trust a citizen may move to another municipality.
- Value to society: a citizen has some expectation of what a municipality should offer: safety on the streets, a clean park, a school etc.
- Comparison: rating municipal services is based on expectations; expectations are based on experience with other comparable municipalities/institutions.

We also used an indicator to measure satisfaction at the counter (a ten-point scale performance indicator used during the previous yearly measurements). Ranking the satisfaction experience at the counter gave a different pattern than the total experience (measured by the TRI*M Index). The TRI*M Grid was used to show the impact of all the 'bundles' of experiences on the overall opinion/judgment.

On the basis of 'satisfaction' and 'endorsement', we created a TRI*M Typology that gives a quick scan of the situation of this municipality in comparison with other municipalities. It gives useful indications on what tone-of-voice is advisable in the communication strategy.

The grid shows how the citizens rate the range of public services (parks, schools, police etc.) in itself and in comparison with other services such as services at the counter of the town hall or (only for a minority of people who have engagement with local politics) how they experience to what extent their say is heard and how they judge the result of the policies.

In the first year of measurement only the services at the counter were evaluated. The TRI*M Index Questions were not focused on the service at the counter but formulated more general. The measured TRI*M Indices (80 municipalities) were rather low, varying from 7 to 55.

The typology showed considerable differences between the participating municipalities on the dimension 'endorsement', varying from 2% to 37%. To a lesser extent, when compared with the national government example described before, the top-2 boxes are rather low with direct consequences for the typology footprint.

The overall grid (all the participating municipalities together) looked as follows:

44

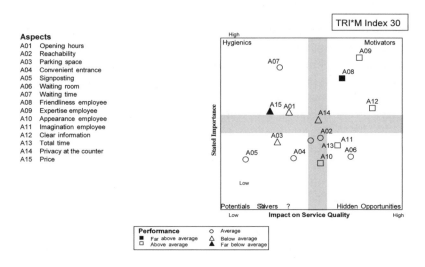

Aspects
A01   Opening hours
A02   Reachability
A03   Parking space
A04   Convenient entrance
A05   Signposting
A06   Waiting room
A07   Waiting time
A08   Friendliness employee
A09   Expertise employee
A10   Appearance employee
A11   Imagination employee
A12   Clear information
A13   Total time
A14   Privacy at the counter
A15   Price

Fig. 8. Example of Grid

Despite the low Index, the Grid looks rather good. In the Motivator quadrant we see all aspects with above average ratings (and that is where we want them to be: good performance in an area where it matters). The lower, under average ratings are in or close to the Savers quadrant where stated importance and impact on the Index is relatively low.

However, the overall Grid is based on all the participating municipalities. Underlying there are considerable differences. For example, a municipality with a very low Index obviously had a problem with opening hours and parking space as the following grid shows.

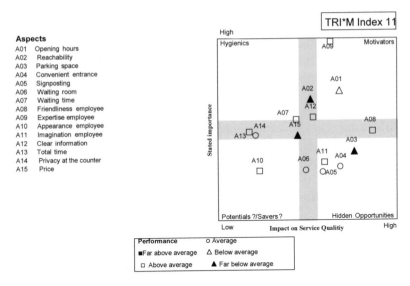

Aspects
A01   Opening hours
A02   Reachability
A03   Parking space
A04   Convenient entrance
A05   Signposting
A06   Waiting room
A07   Waiting time
A08   Friendliness employee
A09   Expertise employee
A10   Appearance employee
A11   Imagination employee
A12   Clear information
A13   Total time
A14   Privacy at the counter
A15   Price

Fig. 9. Example of Grid

Another TRI*M (P&E) analysis showed that municipalities are quite focused: the variance is the lowest for those aspects with the highest customer ratings: 'friendliness', 'expertise' and 'clear information'.

The aforementioned cases are two examples from the national government and the local government respectively. In both situations we are clearly dealing with a public service application of TRI*M. The TRI*M tools appeared to be very useful. Indices for the evaluation of service quality in the public sector are nevertheless much lower than in the private sector, also taking into consideration the cultural aspect that the Dutch give lower ratings than the average European. The hypothesis is that public institutions get lower ratings than private companies. Test results are heavily dependent on the definition of the universe of the public sector.

Because there is also a large grey area between public and private sector, the main question is whether there is a monopoly or a competitive situation. Some former typical public sector companies, for example those in the energy and post sector, do not have a clear position in that respect.

Although by now many countries have created an open market, there is still no complete competitive situation. Under these circumstances former public institutions have been 'warming up' for a couple of years and preparing for the competitive challenge. In this situation a tendency already exists to use the TRI*M Questions for the private sector and to use the benchmarks for services in the profit sector. However, one has to balance this against the practical usability of the four TRI*M Questions for the profit sector. Do the consumers (the respondents) already perceive this sector as a sector where they can make their own choices? Is the supply side already transparent, does the price mechanism already work?

Case 3: Nursing Homes

Nursing homes are another illustrative example for experiences in the grey area between the public and the private sector. In this case we also have to decide carefully which four TRI*M Questions are applicable: the TRI*M Questions for the public sector or the TRI*M Questions for the private sector. We decided that the TRI*M Questions for the private sector apply best:

- Overall performance (based on experience, how do you rate?)
- Recommendation (would you recommend?)
- Loyalty intention (if you had the choice, would you choose again?)
- Comparison (did this nursing home have advantages?)

Although the choice for a nursing home is often not free, we nevertheless estimate that an elderly person and their family are able to make a comparison with other nursing homes, e.g. by sharing experiences with their social environment. They can make a recommendation and can have the intention to choose the same nursing home again (if they had a free choice).

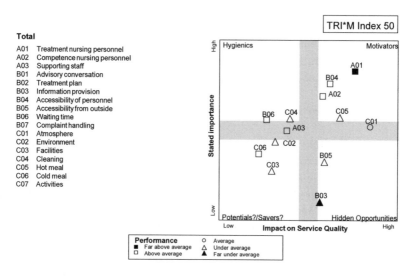

Fig. 10. Example of Grid

The grid clearly showed what the motivators are. The hypothesis was that the serving personnel lacked competence and that this would have a strong negative effect on the overall rating, but it appeared to be very simple: the major dissatisfying aspect with a very strong impact on the overall rating appeared to be the hot meals! Competence of personnel was also located in the Motivator quadrant, but close to the Hygienics quadrant and with a good rating. At the time of research the allegedly poor quality of the nursing home staff drew a lot of attention in the media. Research showed that the problem was not the competence but the accessibility (time pressure, understaffed) of the staff, the latter being positioned in the Hidden Opportunities quadrant, which means that improvements are expected to have a positive effect on the TRI*M Index.

Some other TRI*M examples from the grey area between public and private are:

Service Organisation 'Justis'

The Service Organisation 'Justis' is a service organisation of the Ministry of Justice in the area of integrity and prevention. The main task of 'Justis' is preventatively testing integrity.

In this study it was decided to use the TRI*M Questions for the public sector. The recommendation and re-use questions do not make much sense in this case and lead to confusion among the respondents. Comparisons with other institutions with mandatory usage (fourth TRI*M Index Question) were made by the respondents.

Dutch Institute for Image and Sound

The Dutch Institute for Image and Sound administers 70% of the Dutch audio-visual inheritance. One the main objectives of this organisation is to make the collections available to as many clients as possible. There is no other organisation that offers the same services. However, there are institutions that have some overlap with part of the services the institute offers e.g. the National Photo Archive, the Filmmuseum, stock shot archives, music producers etc.
Here it was decided to stay as close to the TRI*M Questions for the private sector as possible.

IND Immigration Service

This organisation is responsible for the assessment of asylum seekers. The objective of the study was the evaluation of the service quality and the information provision in particular during the sometimes long period that it takes to deal with a request for asylum.

In this case it is clear: there are no competitors, so the public sector version of TRI*M was used. Implicit comparison is most probably with types of organisations such as social services and tax offices. Value to society is also applicable, because the IND was established as a public institution with clear objectives.

Benchmarking

The TRI*M Index gets more meaning when it is compared to a benchmark figure. In the public sector this is even more complicated than in the private sector, because the public sector is more diverse.

The Global TRI*M Centre has a long experience with benchmarking the TRI*M tools. In most cases the TRI*M benchmarking database can provide the TRI*M client with a benchmark of the sector the client's company is in.

In the public sector this is less probable. There seems to be a big variance in the TRI*M scores depending on the topic and the sub-sector. It is therefore advisable to conduct a small benchmarking-survey which can reflect the special situation in each country. This type of survey can usually be held using an access panel where respondents are screened for their experience with relevant governmental institutions.

4.3 Summary

TRI*M is just a tool in the Stakeholder Management toolbox, but it is the Swiss knife with all its handy applications that can help to analyse the relation with all the stakeholders of an organisation, whether it is a profit or non-profit organisation.

The TRI*M Index is a robust indicator based on four pillars, all of which are indicators of the overall appreciation, but from a different angle. The TRI*M Typology gives a signature of the situation a public institution is in: how much public support is there when new measures are prepared? More powerful than a normal two-dimensional grid (importance-satisfaction), the TRI*M Grid adds an extra axis, which makes it possible to identify Hygienics and Hidden Opportunities. This clarifies that some aspects with a high rating should not be neglected, even if the impact on the overall appreciation score is low. Furthermore, investment in an aspect that is not considered as important by the public might be worthwhile to invest in if the impact of this aspect on the overall appreciation is high.

It is clear that TRI*M can also be valuable for stakeholder research in the public sector, as it has already proved itself for such a long time in the private sector.

5 Stakeholder Based Measuring and Management of CSR and Its Impact on Corporate Reputation

Steffen P. Hermann

5.1 How CSR, Corporate Reputation and Stakeholder Management Are Interconnected

With high-profile corporate scandals dominating news headlines, stake-holders are becoming increasingly cynical towards corporations and holding them accountable for their behavior and actions, expecting them to behave ethically and to support social and environmental causes. This expectation applies particularly to large multinational companies which can be linked in peoples' minds to environmental issues such as pollution, congestion and the depletion of natural resources as well as to social issues like ethical behaviour, human rights and labour conditions.

No doubt: CSR is a hot and still rising topic in society (including media), business, academia & politics – some have even called this a *"CSR euphoria"* (Hermann/Kirchgeorg 2006).

According to the World Business Council for Sustainable Development (WBCSD), CSR is defined as *"the continuing commitment by business to behave ethically and contribute to economic development while improving the quality of life of the workforce and their families as well as of the local community and society at large"*. The stated stakeholder groups (employees, community, society) indicate the relevance of the stakeholder approach for CSR. In this context growing CSR activities (especially communication) are shown especially by large multinational companies worldwide, especially in resource and/or labour intensive industries (e.g. chemistry, textiles, manufacturing, automotive, energy) but also e.g. in finance. Other companies are not active or still behave unethically. In which way ever – activity or inactivity is noted by the stakeholders and affects a company's CSR image and overall Reputation.

Typical business questions that arise in this context are: How does the public perceive our company's behaviour and contribution to society?

How can we be sure that stakeholders recognise your efforts to control pollution, for example, as much as those of your competitors? What matters most to our stakeholders and which strengths & weaknesses do we have in their perception?

Corporate Reputation as concept is discussed since many years and its importance is undoubted. Companies with a good reputation:

- are in general also financially more successful,
- have a better Corporate Brand image,
- have easier access to capital,
- attract, motivate and maintain (talented) employees more easily,
- acquire new customers more easily,
- can take higher prices for their products & services,
- face higher acceptance of newly launched products,
- deter competitors from market entry,
- work as a "social insurance" for weathering a crisis in the future

A common definition for Corporate Reputation describes it as *"the collective expectations (emotional and rational) that various audiences, specifically stakeholders have of a corporation's products, services and activities surrounding its business, social and financial performance"* (Norman, 2001).

How the Corporation is perceived & experienced by stakeholders is, in sum-total, its Reputation. As serving stakeholder interests is an elementary part of reputation, it has by the very nature of its concept also to include CSR-related topics. Hence CSR is a dimension or a part of a company's reputation and impacts its' overall level. However, the way in which to achieve excellent corporate reputation with CSR issues varies according to the respective stakeholder group. This is why reputation management is a truly challenging task.

In sum: The stakeholder's perception of a company's CSR image is a strong reflection of the overall market sentiment towards that company. Apart from the moral obligation for companies to address their corporate and social responsibilities there are numerous benefits of a strong CSR reputation to an organisation, that are in line with the benefits of a good reputation. Yet and surprisingly there's still a lack of profound information of the CSR perceptions of most company's stakeholders, which would be the basis for systematic CSR and Reputation management.

This "voice of the stakeholders" reveals much more about the current position of a company in the public CSR discussion than most available rating based on experts` judgements. There is a substantial need for primary research giving fact based information serving as decision support for Corporate Sustainability Branding – the stakeholder and CSR / Sustainability oriented profiling of a Corporate Brand (Hermann 2005).

5.2   How to Identify Relevant Stakeholders

A good starting point for incorporating the voice of the stakeholder is at first to become aware of who the stakeholders of a company are. The basic and most cited definition by R.E. Freeman (1984) says that a stakeholder is *"any group or individual who can affect or is affected by the achievement of an organization's purpose"*. Hence stakeholders are all relevant groups of people who are important for the organisation's value creation, as their input (work, capital, resources, buying power, word-of-mouth etc.) is vital for the organisation's success.

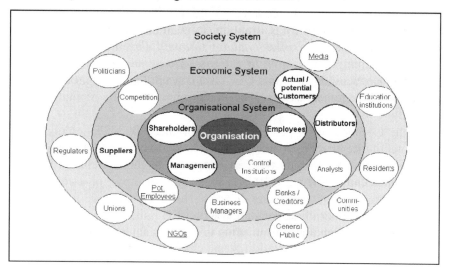

Fig. 1. Stakeholder Model Structured in Three Systems

The stakeholder model (similar Hermann 2005) gives a first overview of potential stakeholders according to different systems in the company's environment. The concrete identification and importance evaluation of stakeholders has to be done company specific.

Some of the most important stakeholders in generally are: Employees (including management & sales force), customers, shareholders, suppliers, distributors, financial institutions, financial analysts, media, NGOs etc. Stakeholder Management as a consequence is about the management of the relationships with all these groups by serving their interests efficiently in order to sustain and improve the contributions (resources) they provide for the company's value creation.

5.3 How to Implement a Stakeholder Management System and Link It with the Company's Mission *

The mission of a company as an essential part of its Corporate Identity typically gives an indication whether a company is already thinking in terms of stakeholder interests and CSR. Most companies have at least two or three stakeholder groups included in their company's mission, commonly shareholders, employees and customers. See Figure 2 to get an idea how stakeholders can be included in a company's mission and what concepts have to be considered accordingly. For instance, for becoming an employer of choice as one important objective in the company's mission in order to be competitive in the "war for talents", it's crucial to achieve a high level of employee commitment and to evaluate your management. Corporate Reputation (including CSR) is a concept that by definition spans all stakeholders groups, as every stakeholder has a specific reputation of a company.

From a more general management perspective, the integration of stakeholder and hence reputation management in the company's overall management can follow eight process steps:

1. Identification of all relevant stakeholders
2. Identification and prioritisation of relevant key stakeholders
3. Installation of a reputation management (information) system
4. Measuring
5. Managing
6. Monitoring (continuous)
7. Embedding into (existing) management systems and models

---

* Chapters 3 and 4 follow to great extent the according parts in Hermann (2006).

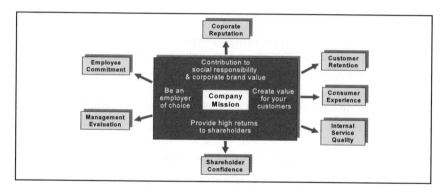

Fig. 2. Integration of Stakeholders in a Company's Mission (Example)

The following part of the paper focuses on the steps 3 – 6, presenting a proven and validated toolkit for Corporate Reputation Management: The TRI*M™ Corporate Reputation Manager.

5.4 How to Install All a CSR / Reputation Management and Information System

Management needs an information system to manage the Reputation/ CSR perceptions of the relevant stakeholders efficiently. A profound system needs to consist of three major elements: Measuring, managing and monitoring. These elements are essential for a working CSR / Reputation management system and continuous improvement due to the following reasons:

- Measurement: At first you need to receive information about the quality of your reputation in a certain stakeholder group, the drivers and your strengths and weaknesses, as you can only manage what you measure.
- Managing: The second element is about managing, hence to translate measurement into action, by implementing change based on the information you received through your measurement.
- Monitoring: The third element is about the continuous evaluation of cause and effect, which is key to ensure actions have the desired impact and take further corrective actions if necessary.

The management system itself has to be based on direct, reliable information from the stakeholders themselves (via standardised surveys) – the "voice of the stakeholders". The system should provide easy to interpret actionable results in order to be able to directly derive quick decisions that lead to actions. Commonly a one-number score as key performance indicator (KPI) of the reputation and CSR image is needed for receiving a fast information about your status and for benchmarking (over time, across units, across stakeholders, compared to competition) as well as an in-depth diagnosis of drivers, strengths & weaknesses in order to analyse causes and derive prioritised actions.

5.5 How to Use the TRI*MTM Corporate Reputation Manager for Controlling Reputation Building CSR Activities & Communication*

As shown before Corporate Reputation is the emotional and rational assessment of a company (including its CSR performance) by its stakeholders. This assessment can be influenced by the three elements of the Corporate Identity / Branding Mix: Active, targeted corporate communication, corporate behaviour and partially with corporate design. Each item of communication or action that is addressed to a stakeholder group also has at the same time an effect – directly or indirectly – on other stakeholders. News about an improvement in a company's financial situation is not only received positively by investors but also has an effect on employees: for example, with regard to security of employment. At the same time a company's customers and employees themselves have a considerable effect on the building up of its reputation, for to a great extent recommendations and experiences "at first hand" come across as credible. They can even interfere with corporate communication and thus lead to desirable or undesirable side effects.

The TRI*M Corporate Reputation Managers consists of three major tools:

- TRI*M Corporate Reputation Index
- TRI*M Corporate Reputation Radar
- TRI*M Corporate Reputation Grid

---

* The following sections 5, 6, 7 and 8 are partly taken from the article of Pirner / O'Gorman (2006).

5.6   The TRI*M Corporate Reputation Index as Key Performance Indicator for Reputation

The TRI*M Corporate Reputation Index determines whether and (if yes) in which stakeholder group the company's reputation is endangered. The indicator is comparable for all groups. Insights from existing theoretical approaches and assured results from a large number of practical market research projects were combined in the TRI*M Corporate Reputation Manager. In less than three years since 2002 it has already proved itself as a tool for comprehensive analysis and management in more than 200 projects for clients worldwide.

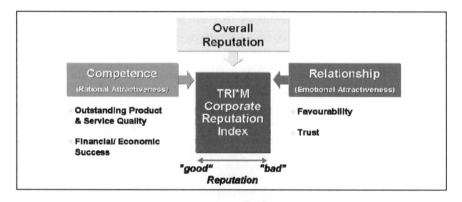

Fig. 3. Composition of the TRI*M Corporate Reputation Index

On the basis of five individual questions, the TRI*M Corporate Reputation Index summarises the central rational and emotional aspects which are equally relevant to all stakeholders in the form of a measured value. It then implies that a company has a very good reputation if the stakeholders are of the opinion that

- the company generally has a good reputation among the general public
- it is appealing to the respondent (Emotional Attractiveness 1)
- they can trust the company (Emotional Attractiveness 2)
- the products and services are of high quality (Attractiveness as a result of Competence 1), and
- the company is commercially successful (Attractiveness as a result of Competence 2).

The five partial indicators selected have proved themselves with different stakeholder groups and in over 50 countries. According to this, the concepts of emotional attractiveness and attractiveness as a result of competence also apply cross-culturally. On the basis of the TRI*M Benchmarking Database, regional peculiarities in the manner of responding can be taken into account in the interpretation of the results.

5.7   The TRI*M Reputation Radar as Holistic Reputation Overview

TRI*M Corporate Reputation Radar combines the results of the Reputation Index for all stakeholders. As a result it is possible to get a differentiated 360° view of all the stakeholders that are relevant to the company – customers, suppliers, employees, investors (see Figure 4). The Radar detects very quickly whether the level of reputation is homogeneous or whether individual groups of stakeholders show lower values than others.

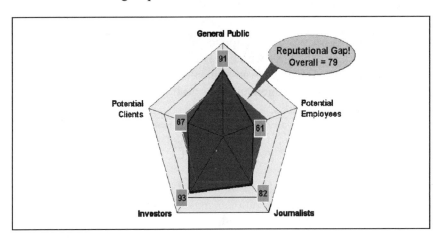

*Fig. 4. The TRI*M Corporate Reputation Radar*

This would then point to the fact that the communication strategy for this group must be looked into more closely and that the causes of the inferior reputation values need to be established.

The Benchmarking Database helps in the recognition of "normal" differences in the levels between the stakeholders. In this database 10 stakeholder groups are identified and systematically recorded. In customer projects which have already been carried out, on average five different stakeholder groups have been surveyed at the same time. The flexibility in adapting the system to the actual corporate situation and the possibility of extending the frame of reference within the time limit are yet more reasons for the high level of acceptance of the process in practice.

5.8 The TRI*M Grid for the Development of Truly Reputation Building CSR Measures

The TRI*M System Grid Analysis makes it possible to identify the driving forces behind the reputation and to derive appropriate communication and action strategies (see Fig, 5). – The Symbols represent ratings of questionnaire attributes. Even when setting up the system it is necessary to include central aspects of the company's image which have regularly been the subject of corporate communication (core values) and especially CSR related issues.

In addition, other potential driving forces behind the company's reputation which are well-established but which may not have been investigated up to now should be integrated, e.g. an ethical behaviour, protection of the environment, quality of management, etc.

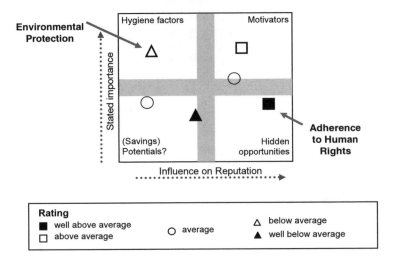

Fig. 5. Simplified Example of a TRI*M Grid (Only Two of 15 - 60 Possible Attributes / Drivers Are Exemplarily Shown: "Environmental Protection" & "Adherence to Human Rights")

Finally, starting from this basis set of 20 – 30 reputation drivers which is comparable across all stakeholders, another 5 – 10 specific driving forces should be surveyed for each stakeholder group. A focus on CSR issues can be used by decision.

The open statistical analysis model used enables one to reconcile the driving force analyses with the perceptions of the stakeholders in the best possible way. By determining the common ground among all the stakeholders, the core values of the company for the overall strategy can be scrutinised and optimised. At the same time, synergy potentials can be recognised in the way things are presented to the outside world and made use of in proactive CSR-reputation management.

5.9 Resumee

CSR is an important driver of Corporate Reputation. Reputation is vital for the success of a company. Reputation needs to be actively measured, managed and monitored especially regarding the importance and perception of CSR issues in different stakeholder groups. Companies hence need to have a reliable information system that supports their stakeholder driven Reputation management including CSR. Direct stakeholder feedback – the voice of the stakeholders – is the best source of information about the company's external Reputation & CSR profile. The TRI*M Corporate Reputation Monitor offers a proven & reliable methodology and toolkit as a fact based decision support for Corporate Sustainability Branding.

Literature

Barney, J. (1991): Firm resources and sustained competitive advantage. Journal of Marketing Management, Vol. 17.

Freeman, R. E. (1984): Strategic Management. A Stakeholder Approach. Boston: Pitman.

Hermann, S. (2005): Corporate Sustainability Branding – Nachhaltigkeits- und stakeholderorientierte Führung von Unternehmensmarken. Wiesbaden: DUV.

Hermann, S. (2006): Stakeholder Management. Long term business success through sustainabe stakeholder relationships, online: Excellence One, May 2006 (link: ☞www.excellenceone.org)

Hermann, S., Kirchgeorg, M. (2006): Nachhaltigkeitsorientierte Unternehmensmarken und Corporate Identity, in: UWF (Umweltwirtschaftsforum), Jg. 14, H.1 (march 2006)

Huber, M., and Scharioth, J., and Pallas, M. (2004): Putting Stakeholder Management into Practice. Berlin / Heidelberg: Springer.

Pirner, P., O'Gorman, S. (2006): Measuring and monitoring Stakeholder Relationships: Suing TRI*M as an Innovative Tool for Corporate Communication, in: Huber, M., Pallas, M. (eds.): Customising Stakeholder Management Strategies, Munich: Springer, p. 89 – 100.

Scharioth, J., Huber, M., (2003): Achieving Excellence in Stakeholder Management. Berlin / Heidelberg: Springer.

6 Developing the Customer Experience Programme at UNITE: Working Towards the Integrated Approach

Joe Keating, Rosemary Bayman

6.1 Business Challenge

UNITE is the UK's largest student hospitality company. They build, market and manage student accommodation across the UK. UNITE has invested £1.6 billion in student accommodation and now provides and manages 35,000 student rooms in 110 properties across 30 cities.

UNITE operates in a growth market. In 2006, 389,505 students were accepted on to full-time university courses in the UK – a 30% increase since 1996[*]. The student population currently number 1.4 million full time, and over three-quarters of these do not live in university-provided halls[**]. This results in a market for student accommodation worth £4.65 billion – which is slightly larger than the UK chocolate market[***].

However, this market is extremely competitive. The typical consumer is very price-conscious and also only in the market for a limited time whilst he/she is studying. In this environment, UNITE competes with university-provided halls, other corporate providers and private housing.

Other challenges include:
Seasonality – Students experience a honeymoon effect when they first move in to their accommodation. By the end of the year, their satisfaction has declined dramatically – and this cycle repeats annually.
Culture of 'living out' – After their first year of university, many students want to live in private housing in order to be truly independent – so UNITE faces difficulties in trying to persuade them to pick a UNITE property rather than a private house.

---

[*] Source: UCAS
[**] Source: HESA data 2004/2005
[***] Source: UK Marketing Pocket Book

Even satisfied customers leave – The market is constantly moving; students typically study for three to four years, after which they move on.

Evolving expectations – the student attitude has changed significantly since the introduction of, first, student loans and, more recently, top up fees. Despite the growing levels of student debt, average spend on accommodation has actually increased (from £46 to £62.80 per week, according to UNITE figures). When questioned about the reasons for this, students frequently give the explanation that they are investing in their education and therefore they are "worth it".

Varied stakeholder groups – Other stakeholders in the UNITE business include employees, who are key to delivering the vision and service required; local authorities in the cities where UNITE build and manage properties; and Universities, with whom UNITE have a complex relationship, as sometimes UNITE partner with the university to offer accommodation, and sometimes can be regarded as a competitor.

In this context, customer service is key. UNITE began business as a property company, whose focus was buying and developing properties. In order to meet these challenges, it has evolved into a hospitality provider, recognising that servicing and meeting the needs of those customers who live in its buildings is paramount. Customer service has been identified as a key point of difference for UNITE.

> "In the late 1980's quality was the differentiator. In the 1990s brand was a differentiator. For the 2000s, the customer experience will be the differentiator."
> Ian McAllister
> Former Chairman and Managing Director, Ford Motor Company

Therefore the need to focus on customers is greater than ever. The customer experience is now a central part of UNITE's strategy and UNITE recognises both the responsibility and the need to continually improve services to customers. However, to date there has been a potential gap between the aspiration to deliver a good customer experience and the ability to consistently deliver on this.

6.2 Customer Experience Study – Objectives and Design

UNITE first commissioned a customer satisfaction study in 2001. Whilst providing a useful start point, over time it became apparent that this study did not completely fulfil UNITE's needs. First of all, it used a very basic top-two-box measure of satisfaction as a key performance indicator – which was hard to link to business outcomes such as rebooking – and which was not benchmarked, so it was not clear how well UNITE were actually performing. Secondly, the questionnaire did not cover student needs in a sufficient level of detail as the attribute set was very limited. Thirdly, the study did not deliver results at the individual property level. Together, these issues meant that it was not actionable. Therefore, in 2006 TNS were commissioned to conduct a new, revamped customer experience study.

The primary objective of the study was to measure and manage the experience of students living in UNITE accommodation. Specifically, the research needed to:

- Provide a KPI at the total level and at individual property levels.
- From a set of detailed attributes, pull out the key drivers of the student experience.
- Measure performance on these attributes and hence identify any weaknesses requiring improvement.
- Provide easy-to-understand yet actionable analytics which could be disseminated throughout the company.
- Calculate the potential impact of performance improvements, at the property level.
- Set realistic short and long-term targets.

In order to fulfil these objectives, the methodology and the questionnaire needed to be redesigned completely. To plan this process, a day-long discovery workshop, moderated by TNS, was held at UNITE's offices. The key stakeholders in the research at UNITE, who would be responsible for owning the results and taking action, attended; also in attendance were customer-facing staff who could provide a frontline vision of customers, including a property manager and the Direct Marketing and Social teams.

The workshop provided the chance for TNS to understand UNITE's business, market situation, challenges and strategy. It also allowed TNS to introduce the research design and, in particular, the TRI*M analytics, face-to-face. A key outcome of this was the agreement to use the TRI*M Index as the key KPI going forwards. Finally, it was used to brainstorm a new and far more detailed attribute set, as the attributes were expanded from the previous six to a new total of 47.

TNS personnel also visited two UNITE properties, to experience them first-hand.

Before...	Now...
Topline Measures	
▪ Overall satisfaction	▪ Overall satisfaction
▪ Likelihood to recommend	▪ Likelihood to recommend
▪ Considering using UNITE next year	▪ Likelihood to use UNITE again
	▪ Competitive advantage
Key Performance Areas	
Performance on 6 broad areas:	▪ 47 individual attributes in 11 broad areas
▪ Accommodation	▪ Importance and performance asked of each attribute
▪ Location	
▪ Facilities	▪ TRI*M Grids produced
▪ Customer support provided by local team	
▪ Maintenance of the property	
▪ Value for money	

Fig. 1. Before and After TRI*M Was Introduced

6.2.1 Customer Experience Study – Methodology and Results

In order to fulfil the objective of property-level scores, a greatly increased number of interviews were required within budget. Therefore the survey was moved from the telephone methodology used previously, to an online interview. Respondents were initially recruited via a postal invitation, then via an email invitation, using UNITE databases and face-to-face recruitment. A £1 Amazon voucher was offered as an incentive for each completed interview, plus the chance to win one of five cash prizes of £100 for the first 200 completed interviews.

For the early waves, parallel runs were conducted to ensure continuity of data during the twin change of key measures and interviewing methodology. Data was weighted (based on bed numbers) to be reflective of the UNITE customer base, with gender and year of study allowed to fall out naturally.

Topline Results

The quarterly TRI*M Index scores for Year One showed the seasonal cycle of results continuing, with higher scores generated in the October move-in wave and decreasing by March the following year (although interestingly, with a further uplift in May at the end of the Academic year, whilst not reaching the original high). The TNS benchmarks showed that UNITE was not yet competing with top service providers, however a strong competitive advantage score was excellent news for the long term.

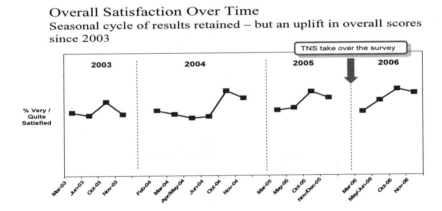

Overall Satisfaction Over Time
Seasonal cycle of results retained – but an uplift in overall scores since 2003

Fig. 2. Overall Satisfaction over Time

Detailed Performance Measures

Attribute importance and performance was analysed and displayed using the TRI*M Grid.

The TRI*M Grid revolutionised UNITE's views of student needs. Location, thought to be a key strength for UNITE, was indeed a strength but only as a hygiene factor.

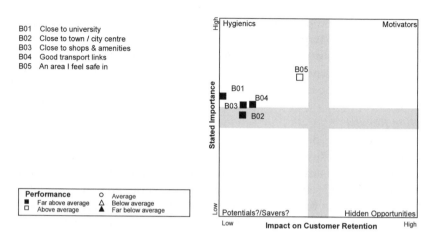

B01 Close to university
B02 Close to town / city centre
B03 Close to shops & amenities
B04 Good transport links
B05 An area I feel safe in

Hygienics / Motivators / Stated Importance / Potentials?/Savers? / Hidden Opportunities / Impact on Customer Retention / Low / High

Performance
■ Far above average   ○ Average
□ Above average   △ Below average
                              ▲ Far below average

Fig. 3. TRI*M Grid: Location

As well as location, other aspects which were previously seen as important to customer satisfaction have now been identified as key to sales, but not as relevant to ongoing customer retention. Typical of such aspects include the common room, gyms and Sky TV. These factors are compelling reasons to choose UNITE in the first place, but other factors are more decisive in determining the quality of the ongoing experience of living with UNITE.

Fig. 4. Extracts from Brochure

Key drivers of the ongoing experience in fact concerned the relationship with the local property manager as well as other, softer, aspects of the accommodation, such as noise, cleanliness and the internet service. Of these, the people factors – the property manager and their team – mattered most: of the ten most important elements, six were directly related to the local team.

To illustrate this point, we can examine UNITE's top and bottom performing properties. These were both built in 2006, are located within half a mile of the Universities they were built to serve, and have 650 beds. In other words, their specifications in terms of fabric, size and location are very similar; however, one has a TRI*M score five times greater than the other. This vast variation in the quality of the experience of living in each property is down to people factors.

This major finding forms the basis of the next phase of improvement action (Phase Two, outlined below).

> "By using TRI*M we have had a sea of change in our understanding of the drivers of customer satisfaction. Previously we tasked our people with improving our score without explaining how. With the attribute grids we know exactly what to focus on and why. "

Mark Morgan
Customer Experience Director, UNITE

Acting upon the Research

Phase One

The customer experience first phase results were delivered in workshop format, initially to the Marketing Director and Managing Director of Hospitality Services. The TRI*M Grids led into an open action-planning discussion and several actions were proposed and discussed on the spot.

Actions taken in the first year to address specific weaknesses included:

- Changes to the Internet service
- Introduction of cost comparisons
- Addressing specific aspects of noise and cleanliness
- Introduction of new communication on rates of return of deposit money
- A focus on delivering a sense of community rather than the physical aspects of the common room

TNS also trained the UNITE research team to enable them to explain and deliver the results internally. These were communicated throughout the company in a variety of ways:

- A roadshow presentation showing regional results for each of the eight regions, delivered by the UNITE research team
- A three-minute video to explain the methodology – scripted and voiced by TNS, and disseminated across UNITE
- A property-level scorecard, showing the KPI for that property vs. the total, and that particular property's key strengths and weaknesses
- Property-level workshops and meetings to plan actions to communicate and build on strengths; and prioritise and timetable weaknesses for action
- A UNITE-branded, TNS-hosted portal where all UNITE employees can access the data
- A strategic presentation to senior management
- A property-level scorecard, showing the KPI for that property vs. the total, and that particular property's key strengths and weaknesses

- Property-level workshops and meetings to plan actions to communicate and build on strengths; and prioritise and timetable weaknesses for action
- A UNITE-branded, TNS-hosted portal where all UNITE employees can access the data
- A strategic presentation to senior management

Property Report Card

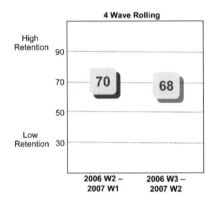

Strengths

1. The welcome that I received when I checked-in was friendly — N
2. Level of customer support provided by the local team (accommodation manager) — S
3. Helpfulness of local team — S
4. My accommodation feels really comfortable — -
5. My accommodation feels like it has been designed to make my life here easy — S

Weaknesses

1. Internet performance — S
2. Keeping in touch with me before I start — S
3. My accommodation provides me with value for money — S
4. Flexibility of payments options — N
5. The service provided by local team helps to make my life here easy — S

N = new; S = same; + = positive; - = negative

Fig. 5. Property Report Card

Phase Two

The TRI*M programme has now been running for approximately 18 months at UNITE. In phase two, UNITE has worked very closely to follow up the quantitative study findings with qualitative discovery work, via focus groups amongst their customers, and a number of site visits and discussions. These investigations have further highlighted the key importance of the local property manager and the rest of the property team.

Detailed comparisons between top- and bottom-scoring properties (based on the TRI*M Index) have enabled UNITE to create a clear outline of the ideal attributes, skills and habits that a top-performing property manager will have. This outline has been shared with TNS and in the next phase of the research, the attribute set will be updated to reflect these elements, in order to provide the fact-based diagnosis that UNITE need to move to the next level.

UNITE's relatively strong performance on the competitive advantage measure is evidenced in its desire to maintain the hunt for USPs. The Grid aids this search, and by looking closely at movements from the Potential / Savers quadrant towards the Hidden Opportunities quadrant, we are able to identify future drivers of advantage. Some of these may be the ability to build social and community ties. In order to keep this search fresh and alive, the Discovery Phase is being repeated in Quarter Four 2007.

6.3   The TRI*M Index as a Key Performance Indicator for UNITE

The TRI*M Index has now been adopted as a common currency within UNITE. TRI*M is part of the language of UNITE and the Index is now the main research-generated KPI used within the business. It was included in the 2007 Student Experience Report, and a 27 City Usage & Attitude Study. A new reward and recognition initiative was introduced in October 2006 (launched to coincide with National Customer Service Week) and TRI*M targeting has been used to set the 2007 bonus targets.

In order to create targets which would effectively change people's behaviour, as well as an overall target, for the first time tailored targets were given to individual property managers. These were created using a 'what-if' analysis looking at required improvements on particular attributes at the property level and resulting impact on the property TRI*M Index. Therefore by manipulation of the data in conjunction with an understanding of how the customer experience is delivered at a property level, property managers have been made owners of realistic actions and targets.

At the total company level, targets are being set for the long term:

> "Our aspirations break down into two phases – firstly, an acceleration phase where we focus on the 'low hanging fruit' and drive improvements that could equate to 5 points per annum for two years; secondly, a stabilisation phase where improvements are more marginal at c. 3 points per annum."
>
> Mark Allen
> Chief Executive Officer, UNITE

TRI*M analysis has also been integrated into core training programmes, including the management induction programme, which involves exercises in action-planning using TRI*M Grids. It builds on and becomes integral to UNITE's 'Customer First' and 'Keeping Customer First' training courses.

6.4   The Integration of Other Stakeholder Groups

UNITE plans to use TRI*M in a broader, 360° Stakeholder Management approach, by applying the methodology to their relationships with their people (employees), universities and local authorities. The integrated approach is based on an understanding that employees and internal processes, customers and business partners are all linked.

Engaged and motivated customer-facing employees will deliver a better service (if they are enabled to do so by internal processes). This will result in higher customer retention, and resulting business success will deliver more profits to share and to invest back into training and development. Similarly, engaged employees will work effectively with external business partners, and thus help to generate further revenue streams and more efficient working relationships. By managing them in harmony, UNITE can create such a virtuous circle of stakeholder groups; on the other hand, if any of these groups were neglected, a poor relationship with that group might impact on other stakeholders.

The TRI*M methodology will therefore be applied in an employee (people) study, and in an external stakeholder study.

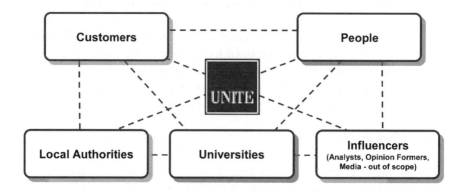

Fig. 6. Stakeholder in UNITE

Employees

As an employer, UNITE has previously been placed within the top quartile of UK companies in terms of employee satisfaction. It is only by maintaining this position that UNITE will ensure that its people are motivated to deliver the standards of customer service it aspires to. Additionally, the organizational changes involved in improving the customer experience mean that monitoring employee commitment is crucial at this time, as Mark Allen explains:

> "Our intention is to retain our top quartile position for employee satisfaction ... This acknowledges that some of the discipline required around our organizational development initiatives will prove unsettling for some and liberating for others. We will establish more precise employee satisfaction targets once the new methodology has been introduced and calibrated."

Mark Allen
Chief Executive Officer, UNITE

The new study will include the TRI*M Index as a benchmarkable KPI, which will also be used for target setting. We will introduce key driver analysis (using the TRI*M Grid) in order to make the survey more actionable and enable UNITE to actively manage and improve employee commitment.

The employee study will be conducted online. In order to increase response rates, TNS will help UNITE to promote and publicise the study internally, for example with emailers, posters and by encouraging managers to brief employees face-to-face. We anticipate heavy involvement in the delivery of results including workshop presentations and 'train the trainer' sessions to enable full dissemination of the findings internally, as has been so successful with the customer approach.

Other Stakeholders

UNITE needs to build and maintain positive, productive relationships with two key groups in the cities where it operates:

- Universities, as UNITE is responsible for the welfare of their students, and also as a sales channel: either directly with students or through nominations agreements where UNITE acts as an provider of University Hall beds.

- Local Authorities, influencing planning decisions through demonstrating the benefits of student accommodation for local environment and urban regeneration.

The overall aim is to improve collaboration, service delivery and communication with these external stakeholders. However the relationship with universities in particular is complex, as in some cases the university treats UNITE as a partner and feeds students through to their properties; whereas in other cases the university is more likely to treat UNITE as a competitor.

Therefore stakeholder study will involve face-to-face interviews with university and local authority contacts in selected UK cities. It will generate a business partner TRI*M Index for those authorities and universities that UNITE has an existing relationship with; and a reputation TRI*M Index for those where there is no current partnership. The scores will be analysed both at the overall and at the city level (where possible), and we will also examine drivers of these relationships. This quantitative feedback will be integrated into the UNITE scorecard and strategy.

6.5 Conclusions

UNITE has shown how a business can use research to make change happen, by implementing a well-designed study in an organisation hungry for data and ready to use it.

Key to this process is the *management* side of the research. By communicating the research so thoroughly right from the start, and using the research-generated KPI as a key target, UNITE will ensure that improvement action takes place at every level of the business. Building in other stakeholder groups using the integrated approach will enhance this, and together they will enable UNITE to maintain its market-leading position as "the heart of student living".

7 TRI*M: Messe München (Munich Trade Fair) – Fit for the Future

Mirko Arend, Karin Jäger

7.1 Messe München

Messe München International (MMI) is one of the leading trade fair companies in the world with some 40 specialist trade fairs for capital goods, consumer goods and new technologies.
Among the designated fields of competence are:

- Building and construction industry
- Environmental technology
- Drinks technology
- Transport and logistics
- Ceramics
- Automation and robotics
- Industrial maintenance
- Industrial properties
- Sports equipment and sports fashion
- Watches and jewellery
- Tourism
- Electronics
- IT and telecommunication
- Analytics and Life Sciences
- and craft.

Over 30,000 exhibitors from more than 100 countries and more than two million visitors from over 200 countries participate in the events in Munich every year. What is more, Messe München continues to do more and more international business. MMI organizes specialist trade fairs in Asia (particularly in China), the Middle East and South America. In Shanghai Messe München has its own exhibition centre together with Messe Düsseldorf and Messe Hannover.

With four foreign participating companies in Europe and Asia and 66 foreign agencies, which cover 89 countries, MMI has a worldwide network.

In addition to this portfolio of internationally leading autonomous events, Messe München offers its domestic and foreign customers the opportunity to use the NEW MESSE MÜNCHEN, the affiliated ICM – INTERNATIONAL CONGRESS CENTRE MÜNCHEN and the M.O.C.-Events Centre in which to hold guest and cooperation events. Thus guest and cooperation events are becoming increasingly prominent. For example, over 200 guest events were held in 2006. Among these were the visit of the Pope in 2006, whose Church Mass was held on the premises of NEW MESSE MÜNCHEN and attracted over 250,000 participants, and the international media centre for the Football World Cup, which took up four halls.

The continuous extension of its high-quality trade fair portfolio (national and international) remains at the heart of the work done by Messe München and is its prime objective. The thematic quality of the events and the satisfaction of exhibitors and visitors take particular precedence.

7.2 The Trade Fair Success Factor

Trade fairs – the core product of Messe München – are among the most important marketing tools. This is verified by a number of studies. On behalf of AUMA (association of the German trade fair industry) TNS Emnid researches the importance of communications tools on an annual basis. In this respect trade fairs are an important communications and marketing platform for large companies and market leaders. Trade fairs are the most important marketing and sales platform for medium-size companies in particular (see Fig. 1):

Results of AUMA-Trade Fair Trends 2006:
Trade Fairs Remain the Leading Marketing Instrument

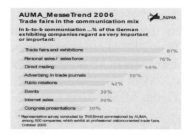

Fig. 1. AUMA-Trade Fair Trends 2006

The reason why the interest of decision makers in trade fair participation remains strong is the function of the trade fairs as a reflection of market conditions. Trade fairs reflect the markets in a concentrated form. They bring together the supply and demand of a branch in one place, in a limited time period and in an ideal form. They offer participants extensive market information and a platform for business contacts.

At the same time trade fairs enable the focused implementation of the entire apparatus of a company. Participation in a trade fair activates the instruments of demand management and at the same time condenses them into specific target groups. In terms of both their effectiveness (coverage) and their efficiency (efficacy) trade fairs are top-quality communications tools.

7.3   Monitoring Success by Interviewing Trade Fair Participants

In order to be able to assess the quality of a trade fair and thereby also the most important drivers in terms of content for the development of a trade fair concept, on the one hand quantitative criteria are used, such as the number of visitors, the number of exhibitors, the exhibition space rented, the internationality of the exhibitors, etc. On the other hand, however, Messe München uses qualitative criteria to assess its trade fairs and these are determined by interviews at the respective trade fairs.

Within the framework of these interviews at the trade fairs Messe München and TNS Infratest have been working closely together since 1995. TNS Infratest conducts interviews with visitors and exhibitors at almost all trade fairs.

On the final or penultimate day of the trade fair, the exhibitors are asked to complete a three- or four-page questionnaire, i.e. in the morning, interviewers distribute the questionnaires to all those exhibiting at the trade fair and the booth holders complete the questionnaire during the day, and the interviewers collect in the questionnaires again in the afternoon or evening. From the aspects of cost and use, this type of interview offers the best opportunity to guarantee a full survey of the exhibitors. This is confirmed by figures showing that in most cases well over 90% of exhibitors participate.

An electronic interview format is used for the visitors. Interview stations are scattered over the exhibition centre in the aisles. An interviewer is responsible for three or four interview monitors, addresses the visitors chosen at random and shows them how to use the touch screen monitor. Then the visitors complete the questionnaire themselves. The interview takes on average seven minutes. For the visitor interviews a random selection of visitors is taken. The size of the sample depends on the size of the trade fair (measured according to the number of visitors) and the rules of the FKM (the Society for Voluntary Control of Trade Fair and Exhibition Statistics). The visitor data is available on-line and can therefore be quickly analysed, so that intermediate analyses can be carried out whilst the trade fair is still in progress and so that reaction to these results can be given.

The results of the exhibitor- and visitor interviews are used intensively to support the marketing and sales activities of Messe München. Messe München is supported in this by TRI*M.

7.4 The TRI*M Index as the Criteria Used by Messe München for Internal Benchmarking and for Setting Target Value Parameters

Since 1995 the TRI*M Index has been used for all trade fair interviews, for visitors and exhibitors. The TRI*M customer retention index expresses the level/intensity of visitor and exhibitor retention at any given trade fair in the form of a single number. It easily facilitates the comparison of time and target groups, serves as an early warning indicator and because it is standardized in all TRI*M surveys allows internal benchmarking at Messe München.

In this way, the exhibitors are analysed according to the indices e.g. size of booth, supply fields (see Fig. 2), origin, etc.; and visitors are analysed according to the indices of branch, size of company, origin, etc.

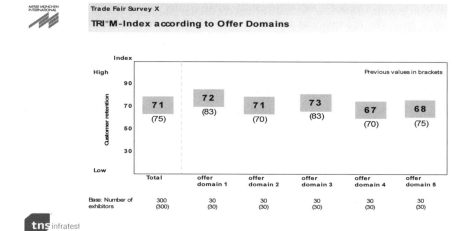

Fig. 2. TRI*M Index According to Offer Domains

The year-on-year comparison is also particularly important (see Fig. 3). In this way long-term changes in the supply portfolio and in the development of economic indices can be correlated with the level of customer retention.

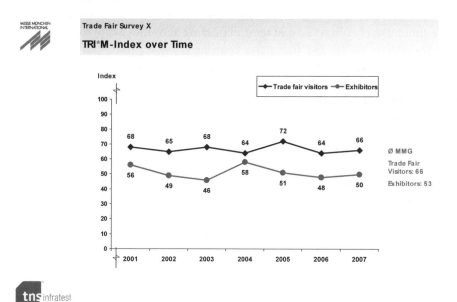

Fig. 3. TRI*M Index over Time

From the daily reports on the results of the interviews using the TRI*M Index analysis, the press at any given trade fair run by Messe München can very quickly gather the correct information to write in the press reports, written as early as the final day of the trade fair. At a glance it can be seen whether the results of the trade fair are better or worse than at the previous event and in which areas. Therefore the press report can be written quickly and, even before the interview and analysis process have been completed, contain information that allows an assessment of the content and quality of the trade fair to be made and is therefore more than simply a list of numbers.

However, for the work of the individual trade fair projects and for Messe München overall, it is vital that by using the information given in the individual indices for each trade fair and its development over time, strategic target parameters for the individual trade fairs can be stipulated and their achievement can be monitored in the next survey.

For these strategic reasons the TRI*M Index is also increasingly used for internal benchmarking at Messe München. The trade fair projects in general, but predominantly comparable trade fair clusters within Messe München, can thus be much more closely monitored in relation to their visitor and exhibitor retention. Trade fairs with below average values can be more closely observed and their marketing activities supported.

This is relevant for Messe München, mainly because the different trade fair projects can be clustered according to their customer retention (exhibitors and visitors) (see Fig. 4). The TRI*M Index allows the specification of customer retention corridors, which in the case of both exhibitors and visitors indicate whether the customer retention is in a critical field. Trade fair projects outside a specified „green" corridor are critical as far as customer loyalty is concerned and require both conceptional and communicative measures to be taken. A minimum reasonable target parameter for the individual trade fair is that the "green" corridor is reached at the given event. If necessary, measures that aim to guarantee that this corridor is reached over trade fair cycles are gradually specified and implemented.

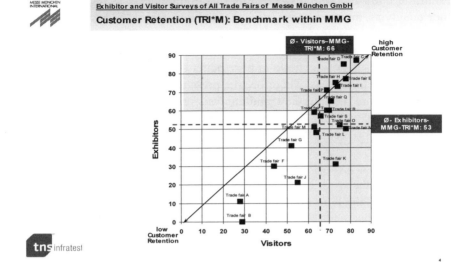

Fig. 4. Customer Retention (TRI*M): Benchmarks Within MMG

7.5 The TRI*M Index as a Forecast of Future Exhibitor Participation

The TRI*M Index also functions as an early warning indicator at Messe München trade fairs, particularly with regard to future exhibitor participation. If a small but steady decline is recorded over a number of trade fairs, the TRI*M Index facilitates the early recognition of a probable decline in the number of exhibitors and therefore in the exhibition space rented and in the turnover in future trade fairs (see Fig. 5). With appropriate and increased marketing and sales activities, this trend can be counteracted early as the budgets for this can be planned.

84

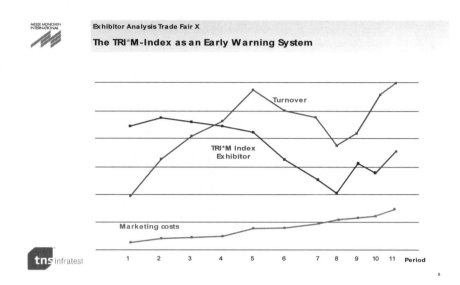

Fig. 5. The TRI*M Index as an Early Warning System

The future trend for exhibitors can be predicted in even more detail, if closer attention is paid not only to the TRI*M Index as a whole, but also to one of the Index questions, i.e. the question about whether the exhibitors intend to participate again. This is done both over time and in accordance with the exhibition space and if necessary according to other criteria, such as for example domestic and foreign exhibitors. When the actual number of repeat participants is established according to specified clusters, e.g. size of booth, in previous events – increased by the intention to participate again expressed in the trade fair interview by means of correlation analysis – it is possible to forecast very accurately how many exhibitors, and correspondingly how much exhibition space, will be lost for the next event (see Fig. 6). Thus, it is possible to make a very early estimation of marketing and acquisition expenditure for the next trade fair event and to specify, budget and introduce the necessary measures to offset the threatened loss of exhibition space.

The repeat participation figures for exhibitors per trade fair vary greatly. The crucial factors for repeat participation are mainly the economic situation of the branch, the primary nature of the trade fair, the trade fair concept and the trade fair cycle. A repeat participation figure of around 60 to 70% is considered satisfactory. The consequent threatened loss of exhibition space usually varies greatly depending on the exhibitor group:

Exhibitor Analysis Trade Fair X
Repeat Participation – Space Reduction regarding Stand Dimensions

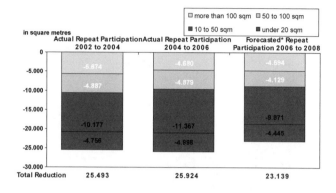

	☐ more than 100 sqm	☐ 50 to 100 sqm
	■ 10 to 50 sqm	■ under 20 sqm

in square metres

	Actual Repeat Participation 2002 to 2004	Actual Repeat Participation 2004 to 2006	Forecasted* Repeat Participation 2006 to 2008

The highest loss of square metres at Messe München occurs with exhibitors that rent between 20 and 50 sqm. Marketing, communication and sales activities need to be focussed on this target group. The assumed loss of square metres for 2008 will be distinctively smaller than in 2004 and 2006.

Fig. 6. Repeat Participation – Space Reduction Regarding Stand Dimensions

7.6   The TRI*M Analysis of the Development of Trade Fair Content

A complete TRI*M interview, followed by a TRI*M analysis, is conducted at some particularly high-profile trade fairs. This is particularly the case for trade fairs where further development of content is required, because they are still new or because the branches concerned are in the process of an upheaval so great that even the trade fair requires a relaunch. In particular, the Hidden Opportunities information as a result of a TRI*M interview has already provided the starting point for greater differentiation from the competition in some situations. Moreover, the information regarding the weaknesses in the Motivator field helps Messe München to prioritize trade fair-specific measures, which are supported by appropriate marketing.

In the concrete example of the trade fair described here, it has emerged within the framework of the TRI*M analysis that it is not necessarily only that the current trade fair concept must be adjusted, but also that the previous sensibly made change in the positioning of the trade fair could not be effectively communicated to the visitors (see Fig. 7, criteria B5 and

B6). In this respect measures to communicate this to the visitors were drafted and implemented. These measures have strongly highlighted the functional, work and business-orientated nature of this trade fair for medium-sized businesses.

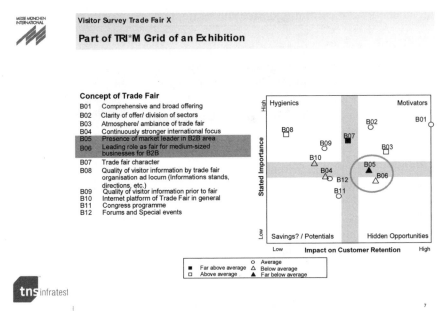

Fig. 7. Part of TRI*M Grid of an Exhibition

7.7 Conclusion

For more than 15 years, Messe München has been working together with TNS Infratest on surveys of different trade fairs. Since 1995 interviews with visitors and exhibitors have been conducted at almost every trade fair, at which the TRI*M Index is always used, sometimes raising questions about the importance and performance of individual aspects of the trade fair, thus allowing for a complete TRI*M analysis. A great advantage of the collaboration is the continuity and opportunity to monitor matters over very long periods of time.

The information regarding the level of the TRI*M Index for each trade fair is spread over the different customer groups and developed over time. And this provides München Messe with a significant basis on which to compare all trade fairs, carry out internal benchmarks and set target parameters.

Equally, due to the analysis of the Index and of the results of the question relating to repeat participation, forecasts can be made with regard to future exhibitor numbers and amount of exhibition space rented. And in accordance with this, the sales and marketing approach can be sensibly planned and budgeted and target-orientated measures to offset the threatened loss of exhibition space can be implemented early.

The TRI*M Grid helps Messe München to identify weak points where change is urgent within individual trade fairs and to analyse the opportunities of differentiation from competing trade fairs.

TNS Infratest's TRI*M tool is a constant companion of Messe München and is ideally placed to ensure and extend the success of the trade fairs. At the same time, money is saved by focussing on the essential drivers of customer retention, concentrated planning and implementing the appropriate marketing and sales activities.

In this way the Munich trade fair will, together with TNS Infratest and TRI*M, continue to shape the future and so – in an ever more competitive world, even in the trade fair sphere – be fit for the future!

8 A Short History of Customer Retention – The TRI*M Benchmarking Database as an Experience Database

Susanne O'Gorman

The History of Benchmarking is said to go back into the 70s. At that time Xerox Cooperation was facing difficulties in business, competitors were introducing copiers to the market with a price below the production costs of Xerox. Xerox decided to learn from its competitors, find out how their processes have been set up in order to improve their own production. Originally mainly focused on production processes, benchmarking has been more and more widely used also for service-related processes. There are many ways for companies to do benchmarking, one can compare industry norms of key performance indicators or look at best practice examples, focus on products or processes, conduct benchmarking internally or externally. All these different approaches have one aspect in common: the overall objective of conducting benchmarking is the willingness of a company to learn and improve itself.

This idea of improving through comparison with others is also the basic philosophy behind the TRI*M Benchmarking Database. Set up in 1997, the TRI*M Benchmarking Database now contains over 12 000 projects based on over 12 mio. Interviews conducted for more than 1500 companies. Many different stakeholder groups are covered: Customers, Employees, General Public (Corporate Reputation), Managers (Leadership Evaluation), Internal Departments (Internal Service Quality) and Consumers as a special target group for the FMCG Markets. The process of benchmarking is highly sophisticated and the task of a specially dedicated team. Precise rules have been set up for handling this exclusive database – one of these rules is strict confidentiality of company-based results: To ensure our clients' anonymity each reported figure is based on a multitude of companies. Each project which gets included into the benchmarking database is carefully analysed for validity and robustness of data. All reported norms are checked for possible inconsistencies, for companies who conduct a multitude of surveys, decisions have to be made on which data to include, in order not to have the results of one particular company dominating the overall benchmarking figures.

This process is completed by discussing the final results with industry experts who bring in their own experiences of trends and developments in particular areas. The result is a database which is one of the greatest assets of Stakeholder Management Research with TNS: it is a database of more than 10 years experience with TRI*M from which we gather valuable insight for general trends in customer satisfaction, employee research and many other Stakeholder Groups.

This article is summarizing some of these experiences we have made with Customer Retention over the past years by looking at our benchmarking data. It describes differences in the overall TRI*M Index and single Index questions in certain regions and industries and shows how the TRI*M Typology has developed over time and which insight can be drawn from comparing the TRI*M Typology in different markets.

8.1 How Customer Retention Differs in Regions and Industries

Already the years 2001 – 2004[*] showed marked differences between single regions. North America was keeping up to the reputation as being far advanced when it comes to customer orientation with Indices already in the mid 70s. Europe was at the time lagging markedly behind. An index of 69 showed the difficulties which companies were facing in not only meeting, but exceeding customers' demands. Asia is showing a similar picture: here Indices reached only 67.

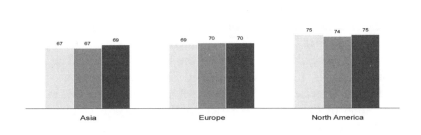

The Global TRI*M Centre   TRI*M tns

*Fig. 1. TRI*M Indices by Regions*

---

[*] All results are calculated on three-years rolling averages in order to ensure robustness of the data

Over the last five years, these differences have decreased only slightly. Asia is seeing the strongest increase in Customer Retention, Europe has gained slightly and North America is more or less stagnating at a high level.

A comparison of TRI*M Indices in different European industries shows marked differences in customer retention. Industries such as Utilities or Fixed Line Telephony face a twofold challenge: on the one hand they have in many countries evolved from a monopoly-situation where the former monopolist is often faced with a lack of trust by the customers and these companies are still struggling to build up a customer-oriented organisational culture. On the other hand, they offer a product which is extremely necessary, but does not have much emotional appeal to their customers. There is only limited room to interact with their customers and offer positive experiences to change customers' perception on the company. Public Authorities face similar challenges: in many cases they have only just started to build up customer-centric processes and still have to align their structures to adequately meet customers' demands.

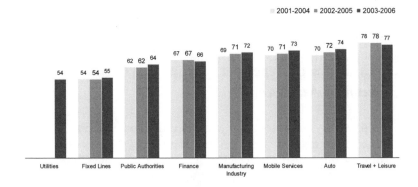

■ 2001-2004 ■ 2002-2005 ■ 2003-2006

The Global TRI*M Centre

*Fig. 2. TRI*M Indices by Industry (Europe)*

On the other hand there are industries who have already achieved a fairly high level of Customer Retention, notably Travel & Leisure, the Automotive industry and also the Mobile Service Providers.

These industries benefit from offering high-involvement products which engage customers stronger than in other areas and a higher frequency of product and service-innovations. Despite these structural differences it can also be assumed that these industries have managed to set up their processes in a customer-oriented way.

Nearly all the industries show improvements in Customer Retention over the last years, but the improvements are moderate. This shows that managing Customer Retention is not an easy task for companies and that it takes quite considerable effort to improve excellence in business processes while at the same time responding to strong pressure in pricing in a highly competitive environment. It also shows that quite often when changes to improve customer satisfaction are made, customers react with adapting their expectations accordingly. They are getting used to better levels of services or products and begin to take these for granted. Managing Customer Retention is therefore not a one-time effort, but proves to be an ongoing task for companies.

The different levels of Customer Retention in different industries show the high need for industry-specific benchmarking data. Results from a singly company can only be interpreted meaningfully, if they are placed in the context of a certain industry or at least a wider industry-context.

8.2 Making a Difference: Competitive Advantage Is Hard to Achieve

It has been widely accepted that concentrating on meeting customers' needs alone is not enough. Despite being satisfied, there is still a chance that customers might defect (Reichheld 1993). It is clear that different satisfaction levels lead to different types of loyalty. Jones and Sasser (1995) have shown that customers "…only remain rock-solid loyal if they are completely satisfied: That is why seemingly loyal customers defect when they exhaust their frequent-flier miles, when they complete a course of treatment at a hospital, when a regulated market is deregulated, and when alternative technologies are offered" (Jones/Sasser 1995: 90). Apart from that, other aspects must be taken into account when companies aim to achieve Customer Retention, which goes beyond Satisfaction. One of the key aspects here is being able to offer a competitive advantage for clients. In mature markets, many products and services are becoming interchangeable from a customer's point of view. To give just one example: Being able to offer good network quality at a reasonable price is not a distinguishing feature for mobile service providers anymore. The key issue for companies today lies in being able to provide a competitive advantage to their clients, to establish USPs which serve to create a lasting bond with their customers. This competitive advantage can be a unique product feature, an excellent service offering, a loyalty programme, anything to strengthen the bond between customer and company while at the same time serving as a barrier for churn. How hard it is for companies to establish such a competitive advantage can be seen in the TRI*M Benchmarking results. Out of the four TRI*M Index Questions, the question on competitive advantage is rated consistently the lowest – independent of the region or industry.

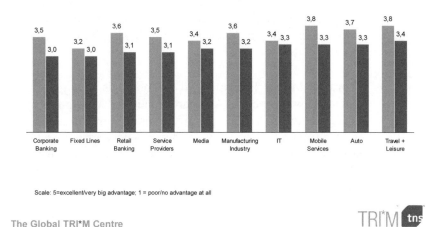

Fig. 3. Means of Index questions by Industry (Europe)

Fig. 3 also shows that despite relatively high overall performance ratings in industries such as Automobile and Travel & Leisure, companies here also struggle to offer competitive advantage to their clients.

8.3 Changes in the Markets – How the TRI*M Typologies Evolve over Time

The TRI*M Typology is based upon an article published in 1995 by two Harvard professors (Jones and Sasser), in which they explain their

94

idea and findings about the relationship of satisfaction and loyalty. The TRI*M Typology is about how customers experience the business performance of a company. Different positive and negative experiences lead to four different types of relationships. This way, the Typology describes the customer base / the business situation of a company with two key focus points:

- Business Strategy Focus: The issue here is to develop the company's strategy to retain the customer base over time and grow it profitably. Naturally any company profits from a large share of Apostle-Relationships which help in cross-selling of new products. On the other hand, a large share of Terrorist relationships can lead to disruptions in the customer base. A high number of Mercenary relationships is an indicator for instability in the customer base, since these relationships are very often price-driven and lack loyalty. A large share of hostages can also be dangerous if switching barriers cease to exist.

- Word of Mouth Focus: Word of mouth is a key factor in driving new business. A key part of the TRI*M Typology is its ability to measure and quantify overall word-of-mouth in a market (market resistance). It shows to what extent customers are supporting the company in acquiring new customers (Apostle-relationships) and to what extent negative word-of-mouth drives them away (Terrorist-relationships).

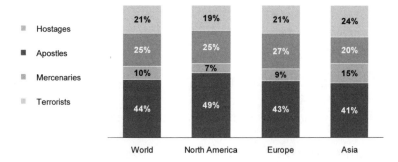

The Global TRI*M Centre

*Fig. 4. TRI*M Typology in Different Regions (2003-2006)*

Looking at the current state of customer relationships it becomes obvious that worldwide over 40% can be characterized as Apostle-Relationships. Nevertheless, every fifth customer has a Terrorist-like relationship to his supplier – an observation which shows that there is still room for improvement when it comes to customer orientation and excellence of business processes. The share of Hostages worldwide is relatively small. Only 10% of customers are "bound" to their companies and feel forced to stay with them despite a lack of satisfaction. This is also a sign of highly mature markets where companies are offering similar products and only very few switching barriers exist. The share of Mercenaries, on the other hand, is fairly high. Every fourth customer is not loyal to his supplier despite being highly satisfied with products and services. In highly competitive markets with interchangeable products, companies very often strongly focus on prices, thereby creating a large customer base which is willing to "shop around".

Differences in regions can also be seen. In line with the higher TRI*M Index, North America also shows a larger share of Apostles. But: Fierce Price-wars also seem to be characteristic for North America – despite the higher level of customer retention, the share of Mercenaries is equally large here. The number of Hostages is considerably smaller than in all other regions, anecdotally we know that consumers have a very strong standing in this region, a fact that might have caused switching barriers cease to exist. The opposite is true for Asia, here the share of Hostages is above world-average, possibly indicating that in developing markets customers are still not able to choose suppliers as freely as they want to, since many times they are bound by technological or contractual barriers.

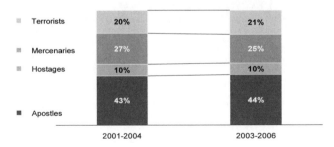

The Global TRI*M Centre

Fig. 5. Development of the TRI*M Typology (Worldwide)

96

Looking at the development of the TRI*M Typology over time can thus give an indication on how markets have developed – whether they are more driven by word-of-mouth or more influenced by structural issues such as Mercenary or Hostage relationships. A comparison of norms from the years 2001 to 2004 with the most recent results (2003 – 2006) shows the share of Hostages to be stable over time and the share of Mercenaries slightly on the decline. Apostles have increased over time – but so has the share of Terrorists! It seems as if there is stronger polarization, maybe as companies are increasingly segmenting their customer bases and offering different types of service to different types of customers – according to their priorities.

When comparing the TRI*M Typology in different industries, it is advisable to distinguish between single and multi supplier markets. Single supplier markets are characterised by the fact that customers usually only have one supplier for a certain product (e.g. mobile telephones), whereas in multi-supplier markets customers often split their spending between different suppliers (e.g. travel & leisure). In single supplier markets the issue therefore is to prevent customers from churning, whereas in multi-supplier markets, companies fight hard to achieve a larger share-of-wallet.

Two out of the three single-supplier industries have developed very positively over the last couple of years. The Automotive Industry

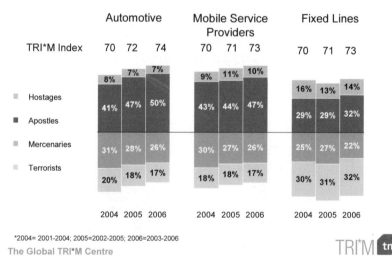

*2004= 2001-2004; 2005=2002-2005; 2006=2003-2006
The Global TRI*M Centre

*Fig. 6. TRI*M Typology in Typical Single Supplier Markets (Europe)*

and Mobile Service Providers have both managed to increase the retention of their customers (as can be seen in the development of the TRI*M Index) as well as the share of loyal customers (Apostles and Hostages) and decrease the share of Mercenaries and (albeit to a lesser extent) the share of Terrorists. The Fixed Line industry has not developed equally positively, possibly still struggling from the heritage of many former monopolies in this market. But also here the share of Mercenaries is currently on the decline.

Mobile Service Providers have both managed to increase the retention of their customers (as can be seen in the development of the TRI*M Index) as well as the share of loyal customers (Apostles and Hostages) and decrease the share of Mercenaries and (albeit to a lesser extent) the share of Terrorists. The Fixed Line industry has not developed equally positively, possibly still struggling from the heritage of many former monopolies in this market. But also here the share of Mercenaries is currently on the decline.

While the proportion of loyal customers is growing in single supplier markets, it seems to be on the decline or at least stagnating in multi-supplier markets. Both Insurances and Retail Banking have to cope with larger number of terrorists and stagnating number of Apostles. Insurances find themselves in a special situation with a significant drop in the number of Hostages. Despite a high level of Customer Retention, the Travel & Leisure Industry also sees a decline of loyal Customers and a rising rate of potentially dangerous terrorists.

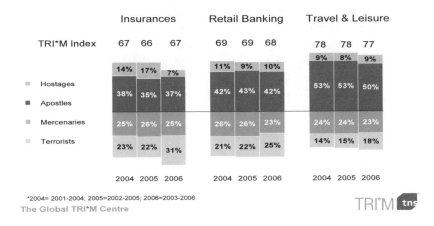

Fig. 7. TRI*M Typology in Typical Multi Supplier Markets (Europe)

To conclude, the results from our benchmarking data can give valuable insight into the evolution of Customer Retention. While developing markets in Asia have caught up over the last couple of years, more mature markets such as North America or Europe are stagnating or only increasing Customer Retention fairly slowly. Despite high levels of overall performance, most companies struggle hard to achieve a competitive advantage in an environment where products and services are becoming more and more interchangeable. Recent research suggests that this competitive advantage does not necessarily mean higher product quality or more innovation. "Customer engagement" is the new buzzword which is supposed to describe the new stage of relationship between consumers and companies. According to a recent survey from the Economist, "Trust in the company is seen by executives as the single most important determinant of a purchase decision" (The Economist Intelligence Unit 2007: 5), other publications suggest that offering "emotional experiences" will become crucial for developing last customer loyalty (Mascarenhas et al. 2006). In any case it seems that companies have increasingly strived to establish relationships with their customers which go beyond the classic consumer-supplier relationships in order to survive in modern, highly competitive markets.

References

Jones, Thomas O. and W. Earl Sasser (1995), Why Satisfied Customers Defect. In: Harvard Business Review: 88-99

Reichheld, Frederich (1993), Loyalty Based Management. In: Harvard Business Review: 64-73.

Mascarenhas, Oswald A.; Ram Kesavan and Michael Bernacchi (2006), Lasting Customer Loyalty: A Total Customer Experience Approach. In: Journal of Consumer Marketing 23: 397-405.

The Economist Intelligence Unit (2007): Beyond Loyalty, Part I.

9 How to Obtain the Voice of the Customer – Experiences with the Introduction of an Integrated Customer Retention System in the MAN Commercial Vehicles Group

Sandra Reich, Peter Pirner

9.1 The Significance of the Voice of the Customer for MAN

According to market analyses, growth in goods traffic will far outstrip that of local passenger services in the next ten to twenty years. At the same time the Heavy Goods Vehicle is considered to be a more flexible and more efficient means of transport than rail traffic. In a market sphere that is at the same time becoming ever more global, it is no longer sufficient to establish purely financial yardsticks for the safeguarding of market potentials, the opening up of new opportunities for the future and continuingly successful product positioning.

That is why the focus on market specific expectations and conditions has in the last few years increasingly meant that the professional analysis of customer needs has become more and more important for the development and adjustment of company strategy. But the "Voice of the Customer" can only point the way for a company if it can be measured and deduced using appropriate indices. On this basis it is possible to initiate the processes of change required internally, although this does require careful communications planning. Taking MAN Commercial Vehicles as an example, this article aims to outline the salient features of the process.

9.2 MAN the Company

MAN Commercial Vehicles was founded in 1915 and is today the largest MAN AG Company and one of the leading international providers of commercial vehicles and transport solutions. In addition to the area of commercial vehicles, MAN AG focuses on three other core areas: the construction of diesel engines, turbo machines and industrial services.

Since 1955, the MAN Commercial Vehicles plant has been situated in Munich. It has specialised in the production of heavy goods vehicles and represents the company headquarters. The company realised a turnover of 8.7 billion Euros in the last financial year. This success is based on the committed work of some 34,000 employees combined with the sale of just under 80,000 heavy goods vehicles and over 7,300 buses and bus chassis frames.

The portfolio of the commercial vehicle area extends from heavy goods vehicles between 7.5 and 41 tons (with a total pulling capacity of up to 250t), buses (from public service buses to luxury buses), and comprehensive services for vehicle/logistics (service, support, finance) through to the construction of engines for vehicles, ships and industry.

Fig. 1. The Heavy Goods Vehicle Series: MAN TGA

9.3   Point of Departure and Fundamental Idea of the New System

MAN is a very tradition-conscious engineering company with a highly distinctive and very innovative engineering performance and corresponding company culture. Therefore, it was first of all necessary within MAN to smooth the path towards a consistent customer opinion orientation.

Since 1998, MAN, together with other European heavy goods vehicles manufacturers, has been conducting a benchmarking study to determine customer satisfaction in relation to difference performance aspects. This survey takes place in already defined volume markets, a streamlined version in the annually changing growth markets or areas of strategic interest. However, in terms of generating targeted action needs and measures, this study often did not go far enough. The call became ever louder for more background information and analyses of detail to help in the specific deduction of measures and/or strategic alignment of dealer- and workshop networks.

9.3.1 Organisational Framework

For this reason in 2004 MAN initiated an additional satisfaction study of its own, which concentrates on the sales offices and service centres and aims to elicit specific strengths and weaknesses of every individual company in different countries. The first to conduct the study were the sales areas in Germany and Spain.

It became clear relatively quickly that customer satisfaction study requirements were becoming ever more extensive and the regional coverage needed to be significantly wider. The originally selected process was clearly limited with regard to organisation and content.

Within the framework of a new tender procedure for the project, a suitable institution was therefore sought that could fulfil the expectations of MAN Commercial Vehicles in relation to international experience, feasibility, knowledge of the industry and not at last the practical relevance of the methodical procedure.

The institution chosen to implement this strategy-driven idea was TNS Infratest, whose bid met the specific requirements from the point of view of the company. Given that it is a renowned institution with extensive knowledge of market and methods and also has its own experienced commercial vehicles team, the rapid implementation of the improved plan, crucial to MAN, was guaranteed.

9.3.2 Interview Content Requirements

The decision to reorganise the project was accompanied by a far-reaching revision and improvement of the questionnaire and of the design of the survey. A chief matter of concern was to establish a company index as a yardstick. The TNS Infratest TRI*M Index represents a yardstick that enables continuous monitoring and has also found its niche at Management Board level as an entrepreneurial management tool. At the same time its suitability for integration into the already existing benchmarking study, which also uses the TRI*M Index, was guaranteed.

In addition to determining the intensity of customer retention, the TRI*Mmethod provides an analysis of the types of customer relationships and by means of the TRI*M Grid provides a tool that identifies the main drivers and key factors for customer retention and – by building on this – helps to deduce targeted action measures.

The study conducted by MAN aims to serve as a continuous measuring device to elicit and control action needs and measures. Initially two separate questionnaires in seven languages were drawn up to analyse sales and service. Country-specific or ad hoc question formulations can also be drawn up, in order to address current or company-specific issues without delay. So that those questioned are not overtaxed when it comes to interview length, additional questions are only introduced into the survey after careful consideration with regard to complexity.

The quality criterion of validity is also taken into account, as the content of the questionnaires is constantly reviewed and only content of practical relevance is incorporated. At the same time, it is ensured that a certain consistency is maintained, in order to create the basis for time series. Uniformly approved questions and the opportunity to be able to adapt the content in a meaningful way and in a well-ordered process monitored by company practitioners form the basis for the acceptance of the questionnaire in the company.

9.3.3 Survey Method and Random Testing

The survey method chosen was CATI – Computer Assisted Telephone Interview. This process enables a controlled representative random testing at company level and at the same time a sufficiently high number of interviews to generate reliable indices at the level of the sales office and the workshop.

In order to conduct the interviews, the events should be as recent as possible and at the same time seasonal fluctuations should be adjusted as much as possible.

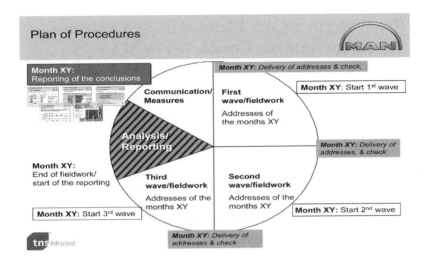

Fig. 2. Plan of Procedures for Survey Using the Wave Method

To achieve this, the interviews to be conducted were spread over the year in three equal waves (see illustration). That means that the customers interviewed were those who had either bought a new heavy goods vehicle in the last four months or had visited the original workshop with their heavy goods vehicle. A high quality of data and results is thus guaranteed, because the interview is conducted as near as possible to the time of the event.

The optimum representativeness of the interview results is achieved, in that the respective countries provide all customer addresses with the necessary content, such as telephone number, contact, allocation to company, in the period being surveyed. A random sample is taken centrally by TNS Infratest. At the same time TNS guarantees that no customer is interviewed several times within one year. For smaller dealers and workshops all customer addresses delivered are often used for the survey, so that for them it is no longer a case of random testing, but of a comprehensive survey.

9.4 Reporting as a Core Element of the Customer Retention Analysis Conducted by MAN

9.4.1 Requirements

Reporting plays a central role in the task of optimising the effectiveness of the Voice of the Customer in the organisation. Therefore important reporting system requirements were determined as early as the preliminary stages. From the outset it was ensured that all results are concise, action-driven and presented in a format optimised for the relevant purpose. At the same time it was ensured that the basic logic of the analysis remains independent of the type of presentation throughout.

One particular challenge was that there are clear differences between the information needs of the dealers and workshops and the requirements formulated by the management of MAN. Whilst on the one hand the concrete action statement for the individual company is at the forefront, on the other hand the multitude of individual results must be condensed to a general report at national level by means of a presentation especially focused on the control tools of the management.

Another interface was produced for the central breakdown clearing, which as an emergency hotline also offers services for customers of MAN. These services influence both the satisfaction of customers with MAN as a whole and the satisfaction with the authorised workshop. Fortunately however, the number of customers actually taking advantage of them is only small.

The emergency hotline is integrated into the overall plan on the basis of an independent study. In this case also the approved TRI*M method is resorted to, this time from the point of view of process optimisation. This procedure produces a continuously connected, holistic investigation of all processes relevant to the customer and interfaces with the company MAN Commercial Vehicles.

9.4.2 The TRI*M Grid, Consistent Prioritising Logic and Cluster Analysis as Basis of an Action-driven Reporting

As early as the stage of the tender process it was made clear that the expressly desired aim of the study was to prioritise concrete actions for the sales office and the service workshop in the reporting. Naturally, the individual requirements of every individual company and its sphere must be taken into account, as every company moves in its own customer sphere and must adapt itself to its customers and their distinctive features.

By means of the relative analysis within the framework of the TRI*M Grid it is possible, both for the outstanding companies and for those in a difficult sphere, to logically deduce the links that bring the greatest leverage for the improvement of customer retention.

In its initial form the TRI*M Grid depicts the drivers of customer retention in a three-dimensional way. All elements are examined in relation to:

- the verbally expressed importance from the point of view of the customer („How important is this aspect to me?"),
- the fulfilment of the individual aspect („How satisfied am I with the performance?") in comparison with all other performance elements the actual influence on customer retention.

Prioritisation Logic

In the company reporting it was necessary to resort to ongoing prioritisation logic in order to deduce the relevant action fields. Core thinking requires concentration initially on elements, for which a particularly strong leverage effect for the control of customer retention can be statistically proved. If the customers themselves consider those aspects to be very important, these elements lie in the motivator field (= high actual and verbal importance). If the customer is still in total ignorance of the significance of these aspects, the elements are in the Hidden Opportunities field (high actual, but low verbal importance).

If this logic is followed, the company should pay closest attention to (well) below average performances (black and white triangles) in the motivator field. Accordingly, these elements have the highest priority when the results are implemented. Average performances in the motivator field and (well) below average performances in the Hidden Opportunities field have a lower priority.

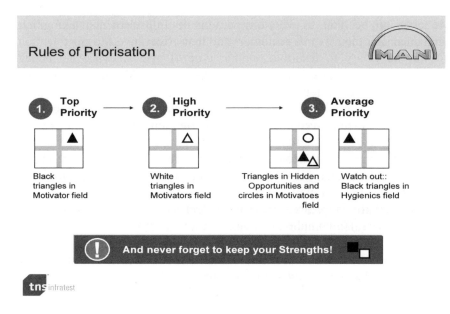

Fig. 3. Priorisations Logic

As well as the weaknesses, the relevant strengths of the company should at the same time be considered from the outset in the reporting. The most relevant strengths are (well) above average performances in the Motivator field. The (well) below average performances have a medium relevance in both the Hygienics field and the Hidden Opportunities field.

These simple prioritisation rules establish for each company a maximum of five weaknesses to be improved and five particularly positive and distinct strengths. The basis is always a TRI*M Grid drawn up for each individual company, which is however not indicated in the reporting itself for the individual companies.

Bundle Analysis

The prioritising of measures at the level of individual items only partly takes into account the interdependencies to be found in reality in the process chains. At company level the action field is clearly pre-structured by the pre-selection of the five most important individual elements. Related processes can be relatively easily recognised by the employees in the company.

In order to be able to determine results for all elements, taking into consideration their interdependency and their effect on customer retention, it was necessary to resort to another type of grid analysis: the bundle analysis.

In the framework of the assessment of individual processes, groups of individual elements were generated at any one time by the process known as „Moments of Truth". These elements show in as much detail as possible the underlying process from the point of view of the customer. Thus a series of partial aspects that are concealed behind the process of tendering such as promptness, detail, clarity or completeness of the offer can also be assessed by the customer. These individual aspects can be combined to form an overriding "bundle".

The combined individual aspects can however be arranged in the TRI*M Grid on the basis of a fixed given mathematical algorithm (see Fig. 3). The value known as the Leverage Value is produced depending on the position of an individual aspect or of a bundle. Leverage Values always take into consideration both dimensions of the TRI*M Grid, the verbal importance and the actual influence on customer retention. Their values are between 0 and 10. The higher the value of an individual aspect or a bundle, the more conclusive is the improvement in customer retention.

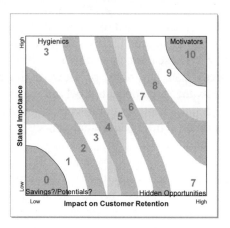

Fig. 4. Representation of the Leverage Values

By consistently using the TRI*M Grid analyses to show results, it has been possible to create a consistent picture in the company as a whole. The following section aims to give a brief outline of the concrete conversion into individual reports.

9.4.3 Essential Features of Results Reporting

On the basis of a benchmarking study that has already been running for several years, the TRI*M Grid analysis tool was introduced into the company and accepted. The aim was to further develop this logic of analysis for dealer- and workshop reporting. This was a particular challenge, as in many cases those receiving the reports could not be personally trained in the interpretation of the TRI*M Grid.

Reporting at Company Level

When the reporting was developed it was ensured that close consideration was given to the different information requirements of the employees in the companies.

The primary aim was to provide an overview that could be easily understood by means of a concise representation of the most important indices and the action recommendations resulting from them. For this reason the reporting is divided into two sections. The first three pages provide a brief introduction to the results of the study at company level. In the second section, which contains 15 pages, the individual results are described in detail.

The central introduction chart provides the most important basis information for the management. The customer retention index of the company and the average of all companies in Germany enable the result to be quickly classified. The quality of the customer base – determined by the processing of client types in the individual companies – gives another, differentiated view of the general situation of the company. In a third column, basis data central to the interview, such as customers interviewed, level of participation, assessment of the quality of the addresses delivered for the company and the use of the addresses delivered, is described in a way that can be easily understood.

On the second page, the individual performance elements are summarised containing four (Sales) or seven (Service) dimensions of quality. By showing the mean values of the company in comparison with all companies in the relevant country, the company can very quickly ascertain in which of the dimensions of quality identified there is most catching up to do.

However, the core part of the first section of the reporting is the established, central action fields, which are based on the TRI*M Grid analysis. Construction site symbols show the urgency of improvement measures in individual performance elements. At the same time, however, attention is also given to the particular strengths of the company. Only within the framework of implementation workshops where there is an opportunity for clarification are the measures to be taken completely represented by the Grid. The identified action fields can also be found at any time in the company reporting.

After examining the first three charts every Managing Director has an initial, well-grounded view of the situation of his or her company. The second part of the reporting deals again with all the questions specifically asked in the questionnaire. The concepts of the customer retention index, customer typology and the interpretation of the individual results identified are also explained on the basis of random examples.

Initially the reports are produced once a year, but continuously surveyed in interview waves. However, if during the course of the telephone interview the customer has a complaint or a call back is requested by the manufacture or the dealer, this feedback is immediately passed on to whoever is responsible.

Reporting for the Breakdown Clearing System

A central element in the overall satisfaction with the service offered by MAN Commercial Vehicles AG is the emergency/breakdown clearing service. In the framework of MAN's own customer retention survey, all customers are asked how satisfied they are with the quality of the emergency service provided. It very quickly became clear that only a fraction of those asked are able to answer the questions about the emergency hotline, because only relatively few customers have concrete and current experience of this hotline or of a breakdown.

Consequently, it was not possible to elicit any strengths and weaknesses in the emergency process by means of the classic customer satisfaction study. For this reason an independent study was developed for the breakdown hotline. This survey focuses particularly on the assessment of the support processes by those customers who have contacted the hotline only very recently, as a rule in the last 48 hours. These people are in the best position to assess all the steps in the development of the process.

In this case it also proved worthwhile to resort to the TRI*M method. Positive changes at every level in the emergency process can be demonstrated in special reports. The overriding criterion for support measures is also in this case the assessment of the (part) processes by the people who have had concrete experience of them.

Reporting at Management Level

Whilst it was possible to implement the action fields at company level by means of individual evaluation and to facilitate the understanding of processing by using corresponding symbols, new demands arose for reporting at management level.

As a first step the customer retention indices could be used to analyse the situation in the relevant markets in comparison with countries, regions or companies. On the basis of this particular index it is also easily possible to obtain a comparison over time.

An annual benchmarking study enables the knowledge gained by the MAN organisation as a whole to be related to the results obtained by competitors in the market. However it is necessary to take into account basic differences in random test systems and interview periods. To MAN, the individual customer interview has proved to be a reliable reference point in terms of size.

In addition, the management wanted to develop the extent of the customer retention as well as the parameters for all customer interaction points. Accordingly a logical and meaningful link to the performance elements contained in the questionnaire was developed in a workshop and the previously defined „Moments of Truth" was specified further. In this way it was possible to measure the customer contact points, which could now be condensed using the cluster method.

At the heart of the analysis is the leverage value, which determines the strongest control lever for the improvement of the customer retention index. Using a correspondingly graphic format, it is easy to analyse complete process steps with „Moments of Truth" at the centre. It is also possible to do this cross-nationally.

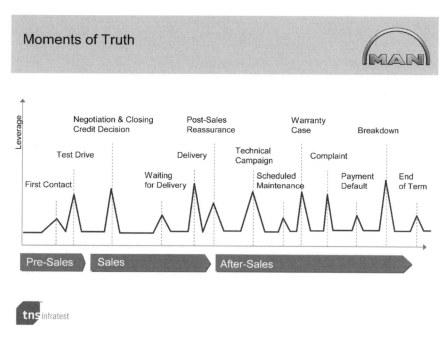

Fig. 5. Identification of Central Customer Interaction Points

9.5 Use of the Knowledge Gained in the Company

The basic condition for the actual use of the results of the customer satisfaction study in the company MAN Commercial Vehicles is that the study uses acceptable methods to determine action needs and savings potentials, early indicators for upcoming risks and the success of measures introduced is accurately determined. In order to achieve real improvements however, concrete measures must be systematically planned, implemented and sustained. However, this requires supporting processes for the roll-out of the results, which were from the outset a fixed component in the design of the study.

The process shown in the following diagram describes an optimum process for the conversion of market research results at MAN Commercial Vehicles.

The reports are highly regarded in the organisation because the TRI*M method is widely accepted. The professional implementation of the analysis

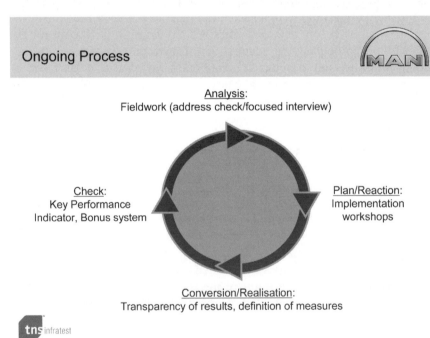

Fig. 6. Ongoing Implementation Process

and the internal communication of the study create an awareness of the relevance and target-oriented structure of the study. In addition to the electronic distribution of the results reports among the regional managers, who then passed them on to the companies, particular attention was paid to the systematic briefing of all management levels in the method.

The first step was to make space and time in the agendas of all meetings, from branch manager meetings to sales and service manager meetings, in order to present information about and results of the customer retention study. Thus, on the one hand a sufficiently good understanding of the report and the results could be conveyed and, on the other hand, questions, suggestions and also criticisms could be explained and dealt with in the different interest groups.

The second step was and is to use the range of implementation and conversion workshops to give each branch the opportunity, together with the employees of the affiliated companies, to identify, prioritise and analyse the action needs. The TRI*M Grid has proved to be a fundamental basis for these workshops and the main link for the discussion of causes for the main drivers of customer retention that have already been identified and assessed as below average. After a short briefing, it is easy for the majority of participants to identify associated process chains, deduce action priorities and develop concrete measures that can be taken to improve the customer retention index. Centrally, one also profits from workshops such as these, because not only the practical implementation, but also the understanding of interacting processes is sharpened.

Further specific and strategically relevant analyses are integrated as special projects into the customer retention analysis and processed in independent workshops with specialist departments. The advantages of this are that the method is known and ongoing and the basic data is accepted. In this way important challenges can be met and improvements can be achieved for the customers and for the companies managed by the Head Office.

The German sales area was so interested in the study that it initiated its own project to analyse and improve the results of the customer retention study. The project team consisted of a branch manager, a service manager, a Head of Quality/Strategy/Processes in the sales region and a market researcher with responsibility for the customer retention study. In the team, further improvements were developed in relation to the identification of the target people relevant to the survey and to the reporting. Among the suggestions that emerged from these expert discussions were that for each centre a report should be made after each of the three waves. The intention is to elicit as quickly as possible both positive and negative developments, and that reporting in relation to the benchmarking needs of the employees should be developed. In accordance with the practically orientated experiences of the project team, improvements and adjustments to the interview logic could be successfully implemented. In addition this enables the study to be established further in the company and to be accepted by the people taking part in the generation of measures.

The MAN Commercial Vehicles Management Board commissioned a further initiative (as already outlined above). A uniform understanding of customer demands and needs and sufficient sensitisation of all employees are key to achieving the improvement in customer orientation desired by the company. Based on the results of the customer retention study, the "Moments of Truth" were validated throughout the entire customer life cycle. This process contains all customer contact points with the company from the initiation and purchasing phase to the period of use and after-sales support. From the Leverage Values determined by means of individual interaction points (see paragraph 4.2. – Cluster analysis), problem fields in individual markets are analysed and substantiated by means of qualitative interviews. In this way solution methods and improvement measures for the control levers identified can be relatively easily designed and minimum quality standards can be deduced. In addition to the prioritisation of the problem fields and the deduction of action fields, the management of the implementation of measures is also an important element in this project.

In order to guarantee that the results of the customer retention study are rolled out in-house to the sales and workshops even more quickly in the future, TNS Infratest have built an information and communication portal in the Internet especially for MAN. By means of this portal it will possible to make available to the employees of every individual company the report relevant to them. To retrieve the reports a login is necessary, which is provided by firstly sending an e-mail to the relevant branch manager, who in turn will make the reports available to the relevant employees. This portal also enables the system to be continuously developed. As well as additional information on minimum standards, consideration is given to the provision of tools for the planning of measures, the integration of complaint management processes and the processing of customer feedback.

Only a year after the introduction of the new system for managing and controlling customer relationships, the considerable effect that the systematic roll-out of „voice of the customer" has already had can be seen in many activities and initiatives within MAN. Three countries have adopted the process this year, driving forward its internationalisation. There has been a steady increase in the number of internal requests for support in the planning and monitoring of measures in the conversion process. Additions to the content and development of the system to make it even more interactive will further increase acceptance. The first tangible improvements in customer opinions provide encouragement to continue to follow this successful path. Therefore there is good reason for MAN to consider that all its efforts to obtain the voice of the customer in its own organisation are a worthwhile investment in a successful future.

10 Firsthand Report of the Commerzbank on the Use of the TRI*M-System for the Employee Survey

Ulrich Sieber

10.1 Rationale for Implementing Employee Surveys at Commerzbank

Commerzbank has to fulfil many different interests and demands to be able to perform successfully. It is not enough for the Commerzbank to concentrate on excellent products, satisfied shareholders or an exceptionally high quality of service. It rather means to include diverse interest groups, the stakeholders, in an integrated approach.

One of the most fundamental stakeholder groups is that of the Bank's employees. The satisfaction and especially the employees' commitment to "their" Commerzbank are a key drivers for success. Therefore, Commerzbank launched an Employee Survey in 2005 as a continuous and extensive process. After detailed screening of existing methods in the market, the philosophy of the TRI*M System – you can only improve, manage and monitor what you can measure – seemed to fulfil the high claims of the Commerzbank as its best.

In the future, Commerzbank will only be successful and innovative if its strategic alignment, its structure and its culture are harmonised appropriately. Only in this case , the Bank is able to react quickly and also intelligently to ever more quickly changing conditions.

With the continuous Employee Commitment Survey, management of the Commerzbank is integrating the employee into the process of shaping the business. The keynote behind the concept is seen specifically in two aspects:

- Employees are **equal partners** with business partners, customers and management.
- Management obtains knowledge about the organisation's current internal situation.

Unconditional support by the Management Board is essential for the success of any employee survey. In case of Commerzbank's comprehensive employee survey, the Management Board was the initiator. In addition, the Board actively asked its employees in 2005 in scope of the total questionnaire for their vote of confidence:"How do you rate the following statement: I believe the Chairman of the Board is capable of ensuring the bank's success in future".

In starting the continuous Employee Commitment Survey, the Board hit, as it were, the "nail on the head". The extraordinarily high rates of participation (72% – a total of more than 16,000 employees in 2005 and 71% in the follow-up survey in 2006) showed clearly that the employees are using the opportunity to to communicate their perspective, opinions, ideas and comments to the management. Thus the employees have demonstrated that they want to be an active part of Commerzbank and take the opportunity of shaping it.

Guarantee of strict anonymity is a further key factor for a successful survey. This is the only way for a company to get an honest idea of the employees' mood. The results would be of no use if the employees feared personal measures against them. Here it is of special benefit to work with TNS Infratest as a renowned independent organisation.

Considering the aforementioned significance of employees for the business success of Commerzbank and also the general readiness of the employees to get involved with the business (as can be seen by the high response in completing surveys for Commerzbank), it is remarkable that only 28% of businesses carry out an annual employee attitude survey (acc. to Hewitt/Kienbaum-Trends 2007).

10.2 Employee Surveys at Commerzbank

The Management of the Commerzbank opted for a combined survey method. The solidarity of employees with Commerzbank – the commitment – is surveyed annually. Every three years this survey is extended by further factors. Thus it asks in a two-stage system what subjective importance each individual aspect of the employment has (eg: work environment, remuneration/ bonuses, work-life balance, etc). Then it asks to what extent Commerzbank as an employer fulfils these individual aspects. By comparing both sets of results, the action needed by Commerzbank is calculated. In the first survey in 2005, the process was begun with a "big" survey. In 2006 a "little" survey was carried out, which concentrated on measuring the Organisational Commitment Index (OCI). Thus both years can be seen as pilots studies.

This combined approach enables two essential procedure variants:

- Detailed analysis through extensive surveying (every three years) with follow-up formulation and implementation of measures
- Annual information on employee commitment`s development

In addition to this approach, the continuity also enables possibilities for improvements to be made in the survey process as such.

10.3 Experience with the Survey Process

The areas in which the Bank has made improvements or changes related to the procedure are detailed below. Thus for the 2006 survey the following aspects of the survey on the need for improvement or adjustment were analysed:

- Composition/ structure
- Organisational mapping
- Report on findings
- Reporting
- Results analysis
- Communication

  1. Employee survey's process
  2. Results

Apart from integrating empirical values into the follow-up survey, it was also necessary to change the process due to the differential focus of the survey ("big" versus "small" survey).

Composition / Structure

For the first survey in 2005 the Bank had already opted to use an online questionnaire which was hosted by the secure server of TNS Infratest. A Hotline specifically provided for the Employee Survey ensured that all the employees' questions concerning this survey – both about the online tool and its content – were answered. Because of the positive reaction to the Hotline and its efficient technical execution, the Bank also used this method for the 2006 survey. The type of questions – basically closed questions and several opportunities for free text statements – was likewise maintained by the Bank.

Organisational Mapping

In 2005 the Bank went the way of leaving the organisational allocation of the Bank's units to the employees themselves. However, there were some flawed responses so that the analysis could not be carried out 100% correctly.

Therefore Commerzbank changed this aspect of the procedure in 2006. The organisational allocation was precoded electronically based on existing data within the Bank's system. In this way these sources of error could be excluded.

Reports on Findings

The Bank had already decided in 2005 to use standardised reports on findings via TNS Infratest. In addition, senior executives were given the opportunity to request additional analysis for their division. In particular, if the standard report points out opportunities for wide-ranging im-provements, an additional analysis can be reasonable.

The 2005 experience showed that the standard report essentially were satisfying for the majority of the units. But the opportunity of additional analysis was also appreciated by senior executives. For this reason, the two-tiered report on findings was also retained for 2006.

Reporting

The Employee Survey was launched in 2005 with the extensive variant. As a result, comprehensive findings/ measures for improvement were identified in all areas of the work environment. Each unit could choose its own approach to identify suggestions for improvement, but based on their respective divisions results.

There was only a distinct requirement regarding the actual reporting: namely that all measures which lay *outside* their own department were to be reported to the Project Office. These wishes or suggestions for improvement were reported to the Project Team across multiplicators[*] and fed from there to the units responsible.

This reporting method was fundamentally altered for the survey in 2006. For the first time, the "little" survey was carried out with the focus on establishing the OCI. Besides the relatively simple process of establishing the OCI, the Bank seized the opportunity to also use this survey result to derive measures. However not for all issues, but focused rather on HR development measures (eg: team/division development, individual coaching, targeted professional development). With this change in emphasis, it did not lend itself to adopting the same reporting method as that of 2005. The reporting of the measures identified in 2006 was conducted in a structured form across HR consultants and not across the sectors themselves.

Results Analysis

It was worth reappraising the measures each sector developed for itself and also the measures submitted as proposals by other units and made available across the Project Team, for possibilities of implementation. For this there was no central specification. The units thus also reviewed different approaches, eg: prioritisation through employees and allocation of responsibilities to line managers or the formation of employee projects for which teams of employees were responsible.

The HR consultants derived particular meaning through the 2006 survey's focus on HRdevelopment measures. As business partners, in a methodical and professional way they actively supported and advised on the analysis

---

[*] The role of the multiplicators is described in more detail in the "Communication" section.

and subsequent formulation of measures. In this way, the senior executives were immediately able to access the specific professional competence of the HR consultants. The identified needs of the sectors relating to HR development could immediately be provided with specific measures.

Communication – Employee Survey

In the first year of the survey, communication was of great importance. The purpose, the function and also the procedure had to be communicated intelligibly and promptly to all employees. To this end, besides the standard channels, such as for example detailed descriptions on the Bank's Intranet and articles in the in-house employee magazine, so-called multiplicators were assigned. Each unit specifically designated personnel for the Employee Survey who were informed in detail about all aspects of the survey – the multiplicators. Employees thus could directly contact colleagues in their own sector with any questions. In addition, the multiplicators also assumed a coordination function. For example, they took responsibility of the bundling of the measures and forwarded them to the Project Team.

In 2006 this extensive system of communication was abandoned for two reasons. On the one hand, the basis had already been established in 2005, i.e. the purpose, function and procedure had already been described in detail and the employees had become familiar with the process in the previous year from their own viewpoint. On the other hand, the "little" survey does not require the same effort of coordination, since no comprehensive formulation of measures by employees took place, but measures were confined to personnel development.

Communication – Results

The unit results were made available by a CD in 2005 to senior management. To proceed further, i.e. communication across the levels of hierarchy to the individual employee, there was no central standard or recommendation. The effect of this was that the employee information was altogether disseminated over a considerable interval of time. Also information handling was heavily heterogeneous, so that the employees of different units were not informed in the same detail.

In order to harmonise this, an improved procedure for communication of results was introduced in the 2006 survey. The HR department drafted a dialogue cascade, which scheduled detailed time frames for information to reach each level of hierarchy. Within this dialogue cascade, the HR consultants advised on the process in their role as business partners. This meant in detail that the senior executives formulated the optimal employee information procedures for their unit together with the HR consultants.

In conclusion, the HR consultants as business partners took on an essential role in an enduring employee survey process. It is obvious that HR consultants cannot increase the OCI of the units alone, as individual structures and the respective work environment play a considerable part – but with accompanying measures and individually tailored advice, HR consultants can accompany and support the senior executives on their way to increasing the OCI.

In detail, the HR consultants could, through active counselling on the ranges of duty named below, have a considerable hand in supporting the results of the Employee Survey with lasting measures and effective supporting of the senior executives.

- Joint analysis and interpretation of the results with senior executives.
- Advice to senior executives during professional development measures for increasing the OCI.
- Support during implementation of measures for professional development.
- Advice to senior executives with regard to the communication processes.
- Support through structured reporting.

10.4   Results of the Employee Survey

In principle, the bottom-up process of the "big" survey in 2005 produced three clusters as identified measures.

Individual Spheres of Action

Measures belonging to this category were not reported to the Project Team. The implementation of the proposals was examined and effected internally – in the respective unit itself. For example ideas for the introduction of weekly team discussions or standardised rounds of feedback were concerned here. Such changes are obviously of great importance for the employees affected, but can be made without the support of other departments.

Department-Specific Spheres of Action

Into this cluster fall those measures which deal with weaknesses and fit precisely in a department's field of application. An obvious example of this could be the quality of office cleaning. Here an actual contact within the Bank is responsible, i.e. the housekeeping department. Or for example a request for an inspection of the pay structure and benefits: The HR department is responsible for this throughout the Bank.

Bank-wide Spheres of Action

Statements which transcend individual ranges of duty fall into this third category. Details that impact the business culture or strategy for example count as bank-wide spheres of action.

A total of 274 cross-departmental or bank wide measures were developed from the "big" survey in 2005. The following were identified as the most important spheres of action:

- Strategy
- HR development / management
- Market and customer orientation

This clearly shows the high importance of these areas for the employees, and also their desire to actively participate in strategic and comprehensive issues.

Besides these three most strongly listed spheres of action, the following primary topics were mentioned:

- Pay structure and benefits
- Work hours
- Knowledge transfer
- IT that is more efficient and meets requirements

This list clearly demonstrates the broad spectrum of measures developed.

From the follow-up survey in 2006, as previously mentioned, no extensive measures were formulated because of the focused "OCI" adjustment. Besides professional development measures, which were derived individually from the results in consultation and tailored to demand, the senior executives were able however to derive a comparison with the previous year for the first time. Not only exclusively on the basis of the alteration of the OCI itself, but also based on a benchmarking made available by the HR consultants. "Learning from the Best" takes centre stage in the "little" survey. The HR consultants actively assisted through comparison of professional development measures already activated in the previous year and their effect on the OCI development, i.e. by determination of the so-called Best Practice Units. Not only the units with the highest OCI value are considered as Best Practice, but rather those units also show Best Practice that could improve their OCI the most. Based on successful concepts of Best Practice units, appropriate measures could be pushed through in other unts as well.

10.5 Forecast

The Employee Survey is indispensable as a transparent strengths/ weaknesses analysis. The active participation of employees as important stakeholders in the shaping of the business is a considerable step towards improving the business culture and with it the efficiency of an organisation. A substantial prerequisite for an enduring and successful survey with the unrestricted acceptance of the employees is how seriously it is analysed. In keeping with the TRI*M slogan "you can only manage and monitor what you can measure", individual steps must be tracked consistently. Apart from the development of measures, which is described in detail under Heading 4 *Results of the Employee Survey*, the Bank integrates the survey instrument into daily working life and thereby emphatically underlines the seriousness of the whole process. In this way for example the OCI values are an integrated part of the holistic HR management instrument of the Commerzbank.

In 2007 the Commerzbank carried out a further "little" survey. In the following year 2008 a "big" survey will take place anew with an extensive follow-up strengths/weaknesses analysis analogous to the procedure in 2005. For the first time, the domestic subsidiaries of the Bank then will be integrated into the survey.

Experience and in particular the plurality of measures developed show that the Employee Survey can contribute to the success of the company.

Commerzbank will continue along this path and use the results as an opportunity for optimisation and improvement. At the same time it is important that an employee survey is not limited to a one-off, but must be updated in a continuous process. Only in this way can we follow the thought that Henry Ford appositely formulated in one of his quotations as follows: "Coming together is a beginning, staying together is progress, and working together is success!"

11 Monitoring of Transformation Processes Using the TRI*M Method

Wolfgang Werner

11.1 Introduction

At the start of 2001, Degussa AG was newly created as a consortium from the corporates Degussa AG (original), Hüls AG and SKW AG. It became one of the largest Specialty Chemicals companies in the world and is now a major part of Evonik Industries. The consolidation of personnel from long-established, independent and successful former companies into the new Degussa was accompanied by numerous integration activities. One of these was the early implementation of an employee survey. From the very outset, it was designed as a communication and measuring tool in the integration process and over the years became synonymous with the process itself.

In the following article, firstly the integration of the survey into the complete process of integration and company development is described. Different approaches to handling the survey results and the effect on (local) organisation are described by means of case studies from various locations. As deep insights into particular organisational units and their specific problems are also given in individual cases, data of all case studies are real, but their origin have been made irrecognisable.

The concluding deductions from the research are to be assessed to some extent as hypotheses and attempts at explanation. They are intended rather to invite discussion than provide definitive answers.

11.2 Approach and Methodology

When preparing the first survey in 2001, various market research companies were looked at. Special attention was paid in the selection to the following aspects:

- Is a meaningful and easily communicable description of the progress of integration achieved?
- Is the method of mobilising senior management and employees appropriate?
- Does it supply a comprehensible analysis of the local potential for improvement?
- Can priorities in the improvement procedures be easily re-cognised?

Apart from these methodological constraints, further demands were made of the employee survey providers, as a result of Degussa's particular situation. As a post-merger effect had to be achieved with regard to integration, a special effort was made to reach every single employee. This meant there were considerable logistical challenges to be overcome.

Since Degussa was then active in 60 or so countries with around 50,000 employees, there were almost 300 locations to be reached. As far as possible, employees were to be addressed in their mother tongue and should be able to fill out the questionnaires in a language familiar to them.

Next on the wish list was receiving international comparison values in the key data, to be able to classify and evaluate possible country-specific characteristics or cultural differences. This latter point, originally not a focus of the selection procedure, turned out to be particularly important in the course of the next few years.

At that time, TNS Infratest was chosen and this provider was also retained for the subsequent surveys. The decisive factors were proven experience of international large-scale projects and a well-designed and communicable evaluation procedure.

This so-called TRI*M Method is based on three elements (Fig. 1):

- The Commitment Index, a classification of key data used amongst other things as a measure of how much employees identify with the company.

- The employee typology, a description of basic attitudes of the employees in an organisational unit.
- And the TRI*M Grid, a portfolio representation of the strengths and weaknesses of an organisational unit. Apart from the actual strengths and weaknesses, information is provided about the importance of the survey items to the employees themselves and its relevance to their commitment.

It turned out that greater effort was required than first estimated to explain the methodology to senior management and employees and in particular to train local managers in its application. In the end this was enabled very effectively, with the establishment of a world-wide network of trained supporters, the so-called "Survey Coaches".

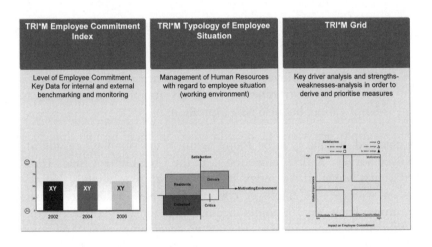

Fig. 1. TRI*M Method

11.3 Degussa – a Company in Motion

11.3.1 Continuous Change

The employee survey taking place every two years accompanied Degussa for the six years of its journey from a union of independent chemical companies via its establishment as a world-wide Specialty Chemicals concern through to the central RAG Group business domain and since September 2007 the **Evonik** Industries Group. This development is further reflected in the attitude of employees to the business. From the employees' perspective, different phases can be described at the time of the three employee surveys carried out:

- 2002, first employee survey: Scepticism about the new Degussa; but also increasing sense of optimism.

- 2004, second employee survey: Start of identification with the new Degussa; pride in achievements so far; confidence in the future.

- 2006, third employee survey: Acceptance of and integration into RAG is agreed; renewed concern for the future; decreasing identification, but also new aspirations.

This changed attitude is to be found again in the summary results of the employee survey. A first indication is in the Commitment Index (Fig. 2). After a first value of 56 index points, at that time slightly below the industrial average, the employee commitment rises in 2004 to almost 60, then drops back to 56 points again. It becomes yet clearer in the commitment of managers. Here in 2004 an acceptable value of 64 points is reached and also the value sinks again here with the 2006 survey.

It should be mentioned at this point, without going into further detail, that the commitment values for the management staff did not correspond with the expectations of the company's board of management. On the basis of the "Benchmarks" supplied by TNS Infratest (industry- and nation-wide average values), values above 70 are attainable and typical for a motivated leadership team.

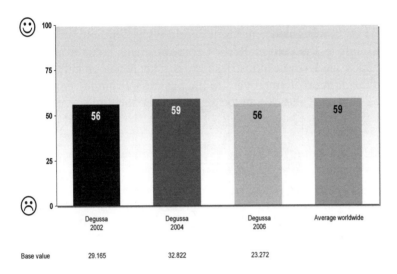

Fig. 2. Commitment Index 2002 to 2006, Degussa Overall

The same conclusions as with the Commitment Indices can also be derived from the TRI*M Typology for the management (Fig. 3). The four basic types of employee attitude are shown in the illustration for the years 2002, 2004 and 2006. The so-called "drivers" increased from 19 to 25% and in 2006 fell back again to 20%. At the same time, the critical basic attitude ("Critics") has tended to strengthen over the years.

132

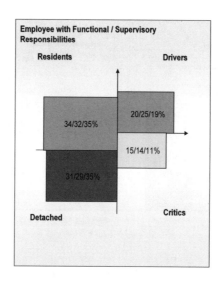

Fig. 3. TRI*M Typology for Employees with Funktional / Supervisory Responsibilities 2006/2004/2002, Degussa Overall

11.3.2   Degussa's Strengths and Weaknesses

After every survey, the results were analysed, consolidated and presented to the management with recommendations. At this point, special thanks are due to Dr J. Scharioth as a recognised and much appreciated expert, who has commented on the analysis after every survey at the Degussa board meeting.

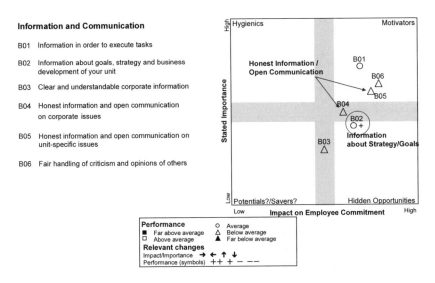

Information and Communication

B01   Information in order to execute tasks

B02   Information about goals, strategy and business development of your unit

B03   Clear and understandable corporate information

B04   Honest information and open communication on corporate issues

B05   Honest information and open communication on unit-specific issues

B06   Fair handling of criticism and opinions of others

Fig. 4. TRI*M Grid, Communication, Degussa Overall

The TRI*M Grid design has proved particularly helpful, visualising virtually at first sight the most important areas for action. Fig. 4 shows an example of the "Communication" range of questions. Here open and honest communication is shown as an important deficit, with which employees are less content (below average). At the same time improvements are shown in the communication of strategy and goals.

During the analysis of the data, there is also great emphasis put on the identification of strengths. From experience, it is often easier to be dealing with measures for strengths than with weaknesses not remediable at the time. Fig. 5 shows an example from the last Degussa survey in 2006. It is easy to see that working conditions, independence and safety at work are amongst the positive points for Degussa.

134

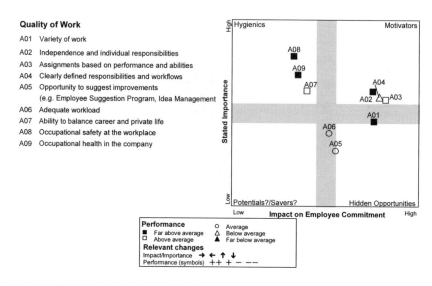

Fig. 5. TRI*M Grid, Quality of Work, Degussa Overall

11.3.3 Corporate Measures and Their Effects

After the presentation of the results, there was an examination as to which corporate management information can be derived and what central measures must be tackled. As is the case for many other companies, the topics of "communication" and "leadership" are in the forefront of company-wide improvements.

Decentral measures were developed alongside central corporate activities. Up to 500 on-site measures for improvement were derived from the survey results by those in charge at the locations and sites. Fig. 6 gives an overview of which topics were concretely tackled. Besides the always relevant topics "information" and "communication", locally "income, workplace safety and continuing personal development"are the preferred topics for improvement. It is remarkable that the topic of leadership has increased in importance from 8% (2004) to 22% (2006) of all measures.

Distribution of Measures onto the Topical Areas

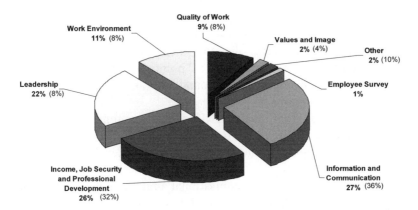

Fig. 6. Improvement Measures Derived from the Survey 2006 (2004), Worldwide

It should just be mentioned at this point that the survey results are to a great extent used for the development and advancement of the company's HR strategy and, beyond this, are a source of the top management's rapid and compact information about the status of regions, sites and functional sectors.

11.4 TRI*M – Examples from Degussa Organisational Units

It is not surprising that local results and the overall results for the company might differ considerably. Employee survey results, as an expression of opinion of the employees concerned, are predominantly determined by local occurrences and site- or branch-related strengths and weaknesses. The application of TRI*M Method and its effectiveness can be well pursued on the basis of concrete examples from straightforward organisational units.

136

11.4.1 Location in Germany

The first example, a German location with less than 1000 employees, is characterised by the fact that in opposition to the trend at the time in question a clear jump in commitment was achieved, from 51 index points in 2002 to 73 points in 2006 (Fig. 7). This development occurred equally with employees who had leadership responsibility and with those without. It is particularly noteworthy that this location has a high proportion of industrial shift-workers who average 70 points for commitment. Values for Degussa in Germany are typically around 50 points.

All survey data as well as the TRI*M Grid exampled on the topic of image/value (Fig. 8) point to the fact that a self-confident, motivated organisation with mostly contented employees has developed here.

Such a change in a larger organisational unit in a short time does not normally result from smaller, continuous improvements. The causes frequently are changes in leadership or radical organisational realignments. In the example at hand, one can trace the successful attempt to change the labour organisation to self-directed work teams.

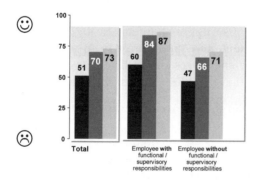

Fig. 7. Commitment Index 2002 – 2006, German Location

Values and Image

F01   Social and environmental responsibilities of Degussa

F02   Appreciation and respect for diversity (culture, nationality, gender, origin) at Degussa

F03   Quality of Degussa products and services

F04   Market and customer orientation of Degussa

F05   Innovation and progressiveness of Degussa

F06   Public image of Degussa

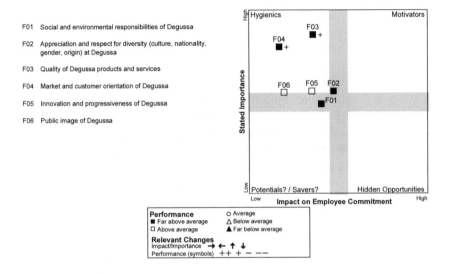

Fig. 8. TRI*M Grid, German Location

11.4.2   Location in USA

In this medium-sized location the same basic tendencies show up as in the company as a whole: an initial rise in commitment up to 2004, then a decline (Fig. 9). This development runs the same way in all employee groups evaluated. Apart from the employees shown here with and without professional or leadership functions, further groups are evaluated as a matter of principle: hourly workers, non exempt employees, exempt employees, employees in marketing/sales, production, research and development and administration, as well as employees with varying lengths of membership in the firm. The specific information gained thereby is used to enable recognition and further analysis of potential problem groups. For example, with the 2006 survey the need for improvement in the sales organisation was obvious.

138

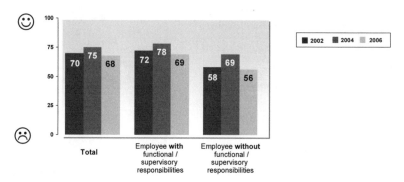

Fig. 9. Commitment Index 2006/2004/2002, USA Location

In the American location used as an example, commitment has clearly fallen, although the reason is not immediately apparent from the detailed data. Improvements show rather at many points. This is also the case with, for example, the topic of leadership (Fig.10). Here the rating of questions on leadership is shown with dark grey symbols for the 2004 survey and light grey symbols for the 2006 survey. From a clearly below-average satisfaction has emerged an average satisfaction with a slightly positive tendency.

A clue to a possible cause of the decreased commitment can be obtained on the right side of Fig. 10. In the topic "performance-related pay/bonus", which is rated by employees as very important, a far below average satisfaction and decline when compared with the previous survey are documented.

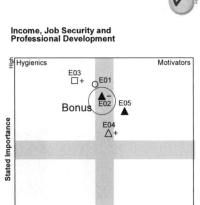

Leadership of Direct Supervisor

Income, Job Security and Professional Development

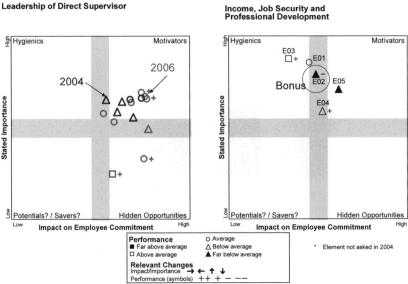

Fig. 10. TRI*M Grid, USA Location

11.4.3   Territory in Asia

In this smaller territory, a clear trend can be seen towards decreasing commitment (Fig.11). The decrease, obvious initially with the management, is carried forward with a delay to all employees. Also the typology (Fig. 12) shows a clear picture of a rather de-motivated organisation. The cause goes without saying: because of restructuring, many jobs were cut. A contrast to this picture is in the excellent evaluation of direct supervisors and upper management. In Fig. 13, in almost all areas surveyed an above average or far above average satisfaction with the supervisors is manifested. We should not seek to explain this here. The example however clearly shows that the TRI*M Method is effective and fast at identifying and visually clarifying trends and distinctive features.

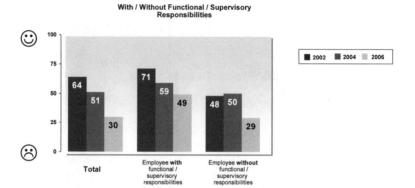

Fig. 11. Commitment Index 2006/2004/2002, Asian Country

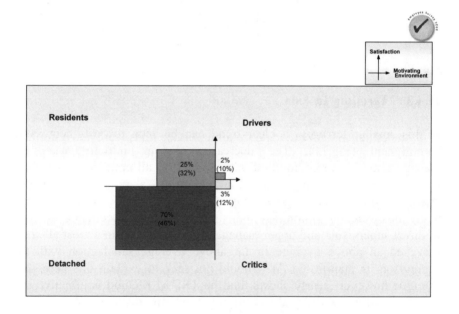

Fig. 12. TRI*M Typology of the Employee Situation 2006 (2004), Asian Country

Leadership of Direct Supervisor

D01 Appreciation and recognition of employees

D02 Motivation and encouragement for employees

D03 Personal information

D04 Acceptance of the role model figure

D05 Promotion of team spirit

D06 Clear direction and objectives

D07 Delegation of responsibilities

D08 Feedback about performance and goals achievement

D09 Appropriate handling of errors

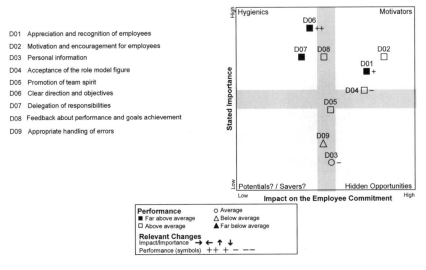

Fig. 13. TRI*M Grid, Asian Country, Management

11.4.4   Service Unit

With the establishment of Degussa, some service units were newly formed. The procedure had ensured insecurity in the affected employees in the early phases; some felt neglected and that they were losers compared with actually "operative" colleagues. Commitment was correspondingly below average. As a result, attention was paid in the change-management to experiencing how commitment altered particularly in these areas, in order to respond with any necessary company activities.

In general, a positive trend is shown, also in the unit presented here although it stood out from others because it had already started with a comparatively high commitment value of 63 (Fig. 14). Over the years the commitment has increased and has also risen in the last two years contrary to the general business trend.

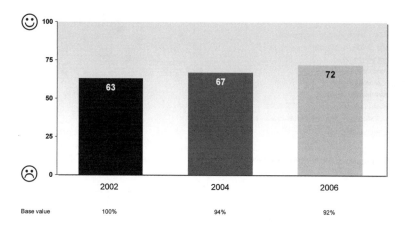

Fig. 14. Commitment Index 2002 – 2006, Service Unit (Commitment of all Employees)

Obviously we are talking about a well-managed unit with predominantly motivated employees who have found a stable position in the company.

The typology (Fig.15) supports the findings. Nearly a third of employees feel themselves to be in a position of "drivers", the proportion of "detached" is pleasingly small at under 20%. Typically, 30-40% is found in this category. An analysis of the grids for the service unit shows some interesting characteristics. In Fig. 16 supervisor evaluation by all employees and by senior management is plotted in the same chart. It is noteworthy that the evaluations are very alike, concerning both characteristics and position of the respective points. Leadership has significance in the organisation (a focal point in the 'motivating factors quadrants'), a collegial leadership style seeming to predominate and leadership is altogether felt in a rather positive light.

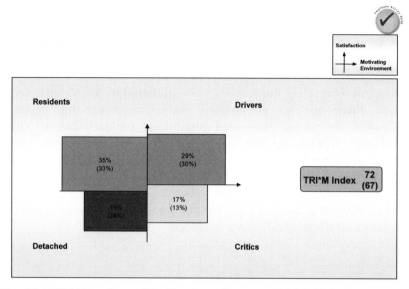

Fig. 15. TRI*M Typology of the Employee Situation 2006 (2004), Service Unit, All Employees

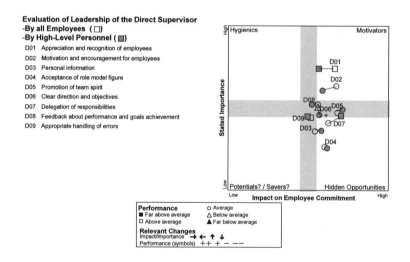

Fig. 16. TRI*M Grid, Leadership, Service Unit

Part of the success can be attributed to the fact that improvements were implemented consistently and rapidly from the previous employee surveys in this service unit. In this context, it is primarily communication and feedback measures that are concerned. However one deficit could not be corrected: the feeling of a lack of adequate possibilities for personal advancement (Fig. 17, Point E05). The illustration shows the social situation: there are no pronounced fears concerning job security, compensation, bonus incentives and possibilities for qualification. These are evaluated with average satisfaction and are positioned on the side of the 'hygienic factors'. Only the possibility of personal advancement is in the area of the 'motivators' and a matter of dissatisfaction. However, the total commitment is not strongly affected by this. The employees appear to recognise and accept that there are limited opportunities for advancement in an ever more slimmed down organisation.

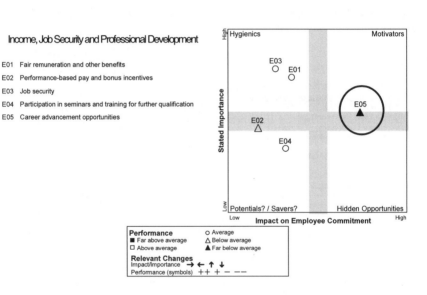

Fig. 17. TRI*M Grid, Service Unit

11.5   Significance of the TRI*M Method

Employee surveys are powerful instruments in themselves for suggesting, accompanying and following up changes. A condition necessary to this effect is

- a clear commitment from management to work with the results,
- transparent results and measures resulting from them and
- verifiable success of implementation.

The TRI*M Method helps with the first two points. It uses indices and portfolios, a language that is recognized and understood by the top management and thereby it facilitates access to the contents. The two-dimensional generation of priorities – what is most important for employees, what is most important for commitment – makes it easier for employees to find themselves in the results and makes it possible to derive the most effective measures. And, provided the measures are really effective, success of implementation is also ensured.

It is important to note in applying the methodology that none of the three elements may be used in isolation. It is only in the interaction of the Commitment Index, the Typology and the TRI*M Grid that significant conclusions may be drawn. As in the examples shown, commitment can be a fast-reacting indicator dependent on random influences (e.g. the failure of an expected bonus). It shows the need for action, but needs a more detailed explanation via the TRI*M Grids. With these, again, it is important to see which topics and expressions of discontent are important and which may simply be ignored. The Typology for its part helps with the decision as to what types of measures are likely to be successful.

The TRI*M Method also has its limitations. For example cross-comparisons between countries and locations with the Commitment Index are problematic due to cultural influences. More reliable here in the evidence are time series within organisational units. Also the relative evaluation practised with the grids makes comparisons between different units difficult. The system is optimised to unit-specific improvement activities and there displays its strengths. This means at the same time that operating TRI*M without additional evaluation has only a limited value for strategic HR control. This disadvantage can be easily corrected however through definition and calculation of (absolute) statistical parameters.

For Degussa the utilisation of TRI*M meant that the employee survey became to a great extent an accepted instrument of management. A visit to a country or location by management hardly ever takes place without employee survey results also being processed beforehand. It is a standard topic for discussion in many management meetings and most important: the employee survey has become the trigger for and attendant to many local, regional and company-wide changes.

12 Customer and Brand Loyalty Research – Two Separate Fields?

Jens Krause, Tim Zütphen

12.1 Introduction

Customer and brand loyalty research are two main fields of professional market research. It is no secret that both customer satisfaction, created by good management of business performance, and brand commitment, stimulated by effective brand management, are prerequisites for long-term profitability. In practice, the two fields of research are mostly carried out as separate projects with different approaches and on the customer side typically even in separate organisational units. TNS as one of the market leaders in ad hoc market research has successful tools for both fields of research: TRI*M^{TM} for stakeholder management and the Conversion Model^{TM} for measuring brand commitment. Both tools are separate in practice, but also used in combination with each other.

In what follows, the Conversion Model is briefly introduced, both tools are compared and the results thereof examined as to what connecting factors exist and in what form the combination of both tools opens up new and further possibilities for analysis.

12.2 Conversion Model

Commitment has now become a fashionable term, and not only in the world of market research. A typical consequence of its to some extent inflated use is a latent wishy-washy definition as well as a sometimes careless operationalisation of the term in market research.

A first approach to translating Commitment into German, in this case does not lead any further. Respective dictionaries give every meaning from "bonding", "devotion" and "engagement" through to "undertaking" or "obligation". While in politics Commitment is understood in terms of "obligation" and "undertaking", Commitment in market research is used rather to describe a connection, however constituted, with a product or a brand.

148

Independent of which of the many definitions found in circulation is selected, the smallest common denominator in all approaches is clearly that brand loyalty in terms of Commitment means rather an attitude-oriented, emotional and thus psychological connection, than it is a behavioural bond, realigning oneself to past behaviour.

From our perspective, the definition of Commitment as "psychological connection to a brand or a product" is suitable for market research. The stronger this connection, the stronger the Commitment.

So how this is concretely operationalised in the Conversion Model? If one understands Commitment as psychologically motivated brand loyalty, then it becomes clear that the operationalisation of the construct has to go beyond the mere observation of past behaviour. It is also not enough – as one often sees – to augment a rational measurement with supposed emotional attributes (as e.g. "trust or "favourability) in order to measure Commitment. Particularly not if conclusions about future consumer behaviour are to be made from the measurement.

Based on the idea of emotional solidarity and its constraints, the construct of the Conversion Model is operationalised by means of the following four central dimensions:

1. *Needs fit:* To what extent are needs and expectations satisfied?
2. *Involvement in the product category:* How important is the selection process? How important is deciding on a certain brand in a product category?
3. *Attractiveness of alternatives* within the product category
4. *Intensity of ambivalence:* Degree of uncertainty with brand choice

More precisely:

1. The *Needs fit dimension* essentially corresponds to the proven approach in measuring satisfaction and involves subjective comparison of anticipated performance with what the consumer actually receives. The effect on commitment is more or less linear: The higher the satisfaction with the brand used, the better the conditions for stable brand loyalty. And the same goes for the reverse: if there is permanent dissatisfaction, it is impossible to build up brand loyalty. Classic customer satisfaction thus remains a central element of brand loyalty, but not alone.

2. Along with this as a second dimension involvement is examined, by which the importance or meaning of the brand choice in a particular market or product category is determined. The strength of the involvement in product categories is different for each individual and must therefore be considered for the determination of the brand commitment on a respondent level basis and not on the basis of brand averages. Nevertheless, the global Conversion Model databank shows: There are markets with a tendency to high involvement, baby- and body care products belong as much to this as cars or banks. However, involvement with media brands or energy suppliers tends to be lower. Consumer involvement with a particular product category has a direct effect on the effects dynamics in building Commitment. The more important the brand choice, the more ready the consumer is to tolerate temporary dissatisfaction, precisely because the connection with the brand is important to him/her and he/she wants to adhere to it as a matter of principle. In markets with little involvement it is harder for providers to build true Commitment.

3. A further element in the operationalisation of Commitment is the *attractiveness of the alternatives*. The importance of the perception of other brands in the market for the degree of brand loyalty is evident. From the point of view of the dissatisfied customer, it makes no sense to change a brand, if the alternatives to the brand currently used are perceived just as negatively. This naturally also applies in reverse: If involvement in brand choice is low, satisfied customers will change the brand, immediately the market alternatives are regarded as more attractive. It is also worth noting that those alternatives regarded as attractive do not necessarily lead to a complete change of brand. A Coca Cola drinker need not stop drinking Coca Cola completely, because he/she prefers Pepsi. One course of action is to extend his/her brand repertoire to include Pepsi. This does not necessarily lead to a complete brand change, but to an adjustment in wallet share towards the new item in the portfolio of received brands used. Both phenomena, brand change and shift in wallet share, must be considered and anticipated in an analysis of Commitment and in any analysis based thereon of potential change fluctuations.

The fourth dimension of brand loyalty is *ambivalence*. This means the subjective reasons, which represent possible inhibition thresholds for a change of brand. So changing a detergent or soft

150

5. drink brand has little cost associated with it, while for example a change of bank account can definitely mean some costs and even, from the point of view of the customer, risk. Besides, in some markets there exist not only subjective but also objective change thresholds. A mobile phone customer wanting to change may indeed fulfil all criteria for changing provider, but their current mobile phone contract represents an objective obstacle to a change of brand. To that extent this dimension is also essential to the operationalisation of Commitment.

The Conversion Model uses its research construct to take into consideration the four dimensions described and by means of an innovative algorithm, originally developed in social scientific research, determines for each person surveyed the respective measure of their loyalty to all the brands or suppliers surveyed in the respective product categories. As a result of this analysis, each person questioned is clearly assigned to the following 8 selective segments, with regard to all brands known to him/her.

Conversion Model Segments

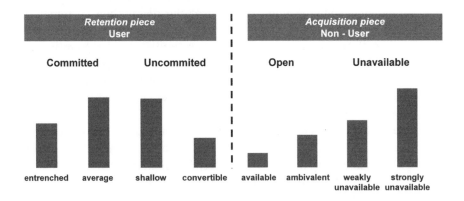

Fig. 1. Conversion of Segments

The segmentation is done based on the analysis of all possible combinations of answers. A multidimensional range is spanned, in which each individual surveyed is assigned to one of the 8 user and/or non-user segments of the Conversion Model on the basis of his/her individual combination of answers, and this goes for all brands or suppliers.

12.3   TRI*M and Conversion Model – Similarities and Differences

In order to examine what overlaps exist between the two tools and whether further possibilities for analysis are opened up through the combination, leading to a gain in insight, it makes sense to have the objectives of both tools before us:

■   TRI*M focuses on measuring, managing and monitoring the business performance of a company by analysing the stakeholders' experiences with the operational performance on processes, products and services.

■   By contrast, the focus of the Conversion Model is much more on broader, softer factors – the brand-driven and emotional aspects. It is therefore essential for any brand management activities.

Customer Experience and Emotional Attachment

Fig. 2. Customer Experience and Emotional Attachment

Both tools have similar goals, i.e. to increase the profitability of a business through better customer management, but different approaches are used: TRI*M starts from a business perspective. Its aim is to continually improve processes, products and services, so that customer loyalty is permanently increased. Apart from the analysis of how business performance is currently perceived – measured with the TRI*M Index – starting points for improvement and prioritised recommendations for action are supplied through the TRI*M Grid.

The Conversion Model puts stronger focus on brand perception, in particular here the market environment, as well as the personal attitude of the consumer. In the long run, the success of a brand is measured on whether and how strongly it can be distinguished in the mind of the consumer from other brands in the market and thus to bind existing users and at the same time win new users. Loyalty and even more affinity are not exclusively the result of business performance, but of the multi-dimensional cause and effect relationships described above, i.e. particularly the perception of all brands – used ones as well as those brands someone has no experience with – within the competitive environment.

The fact that the difference between business and market perspective is in no way only a theoretical distinguishing feature becomes clear if one compares the operationalisation of the models with each other.

TRI*M and Conversion Model Questions

The two sets of measures validate and yet they do not correlate:

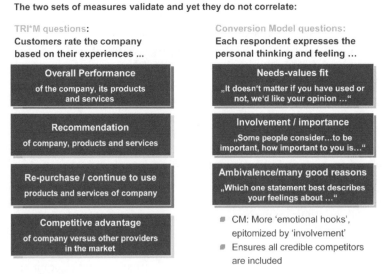

TRI*M questions:
Customers rate the company based on their experiences ...

Conversion Model questions:
Each respondent expresses the personal thinking and feeling ...

Overall Performance
of the company, its products and services

Needs-values fit
„It doesn't matter if you have used or not, we'd like your opinion ..."

Recommendation
of company, products and services

Involvement / importance
„Some people consider...to be important, how important to you is..."

Re-purchase / continue to use
products and services of company

Ambivalence/many good reasons
„Which one statement best describes your feelings about ..."

Competitive advantage
of company versus other providers in the market

- CM: More 'emotional hooks', epitomized by 'involvement'
- Ensures all credible competitors are included

*Fig. 3. TRI*M and Conversion Model Questions*

The difference that is most apparent is that all questions raised in the TRI*M framework refer to the experience with the respective supplier. The question about the competitive advantages of different suppliers thereby covers the limits of the supplier in relation to alternative options in the market and thereby differentiates TRI*M from many other tools on the market that leave this dimension out of the equation.

In contrast, the Conversion Model takes into account involvement with the product category, which has no role in TRI*M, as the individual level of involvement can not be influenced by a company, at least not in the short term. Involvement is a psychological dimension with decisive importance for Commitment to a brand (see above), and does not refer to consumers' experience with a brand but to the complete perception of brands and their meaning within a product category. Something similar is needed for the Conversion *Needs fit* dimension. The question is not asked, as in the TRI*M framework, only about brands used, the business performance of which the person questioned can judge from their own experience, but for all known brands. Thus the Conversion Model clearly measures the dimension more flexibly, and expectations and perceptions of all brands in the market under consideration are explicitly surveyed. TRI*M however focuses strictly on experience and thus the perception of business performance, as the TRI*M analysis concentrates on aspects which can directly and immediately be influenced by the company. In the evaluation algorithm of the Conversion Model, comparison of the evaluation of brands used with the evaluation of those not used plays a crucial role in quantifying the attractiveness of alternatives not used at that time. In the long run, behind this stands the assumption that strong Commitment can only exist if no other brand, independently of whether or not it is currently used, is valued more highly than that currently used. Commitment is thereby more strongly based on the comparison with alternatives and less on the concrete experience of the product or service.

On the basis of these differences in operationalisation, the two models explain consumer behaviour from different angles. So, for example, TRI*M gives a clear indication of word of mouth customer behaviour, which in the Conversion Model plays no real part in terms of in- and output. The TRI*M Typology generates four customer-relationship types who, based on their experience of a business, contribute either to the positive or the negative company success as they give an account of their experience with the business. The TRI*M Typology can thereby be interpreted as characterising the business situation of a company. A positive business situation – and thus a positive word of mouth – naturally

154

contributes positively on a long-term basis to customer loyalty as well as to the winning of new customers. TRI*M however is more implicit here and hence should not be understood as an explicit model for the prognosis of churn on an individual level. The Conversion Model is applied differently here, as outlined below.

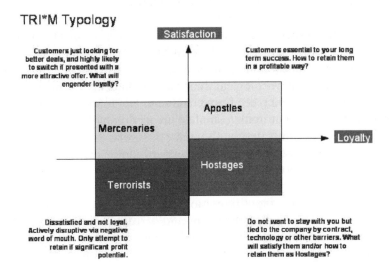

*Fig. 4. TRI*M Typology*

Moreover the TRI*M Typology provides valuable insights for developing a company's strategy for new customer retention measures – how to retain the customer base over time and grow it profitably:

1. Are there enough *Apostle* relationships among the customer base which support cross-selling of new products and services and help winning new customers?
2. Is the customer base driven by *Mercenary* relationships and is therefore insecure?
3. Has the company created enough switching barriers for *Hostage* relationships?
4. Do performance issues lead to a high share of *Terrorist* relationships which disrupt the customer base?

By finding answers to these high value questions, the analysis of a company's business situation assists in improving the way a company interacts with its customers, in making the customer management more effective and efficient by identifying priorities for operational process improvement and re-design and last but not least – with long term research programs – it helps in tracking the effectiveness of performance investments.

In contrast, the segments of the Conversion Model are explicitly concerned with the prognosis of future behaviour. Thus based around the questions of who uses a brand further on in the future, who changes brands and in favour of which brands the change will be made. The optimum illustration of actual future consumer behaviour is a clear goal of the Conversion Model algorithm, which was explicitly validated and optimised in this regard. This approach makes the Conversion Model robust in relation to short-term fluctuations in customer satisfaction, at the same time however the Conversion Model only implicitly illustrates perception of business performance. For this reason, the Conversion Model should also not be used for measuring performance.

Business performance vs. brand commitment – TRI*M vs. Conversion Model: Two different ways of measuring with different objectives and approaches. It is precisely in these differences that the potential exists for a combination of both tools, as will be shown in the next section.

12.4   Connecting Factors and Sample Applications

Yet where are the differences and commonalities in the perception of business performance and brand loyalty? Are we ultimately measuring the same thing? Or does one presuppose the other?

An example:

Max Sample is a customer of the mobile phone provider SmallPhone. He has been with SmallPhone for several years. Previously he was a customer of industry captain TeaTime. After several frustrating service experiences with TeaTime, he changed to SmallPhone. SmallPhone has more advantageous tariffs for his particular patterns of phoning and besides there is always the most up-to-date mobile model on offer at a good price.

The service is not much better with SmallPhone than with TeaTime, and network coverage also sometimes leaves something to be desired. Also with SmallPhone, the hotline is permanently engaged and even if one gets hold of an agent on the line, a solution of the problem on the first call is rather down to chance. Nevertheless he is a loyal customer and in discussions with colleagues and friends defends his provider against criticisms that customers have outgrown SmallPhone, and SmallPhone's service is one of the worst in the sector.

An unusual example: Brand commitment in spite of terrible business performance? Loyal in spite of dissatisfaction? It is possible, and indeed not at all rare. Because perception of business performance is indeed a driver of brand loyalty, but as described above only one among many. In the case of Max Sample, the interplay of the drivers appears in such a way that perception of SmallPhone's business performance does not turn out to be particularly good, but neither is it particularly bad, and instead the basic attitude towards SmallPhone is basically positive. This is crucial: evaluation of the competitors is even worse, he just does not like TeaTime (any more). This may be due to experiences, but the reason may also lie in softer factors as brand image or brand communication.

At the same time, Max Sample's involvement is high, ultimately he has engaged intensely with the question of mobile phone service and some time ago made the completely conscious decision to change to SmallPhone. And if one eventually questions Max Sample about his ambivalence, then he expresses a clear preference for SmallPhone, a change to the competition or going back to TeaTime is not even considered by him at present. A principled rethink would probably only happen here if SmallPhone significantly raised its prices and thus gave the advantage to the competition.

So to sum up, there is a high brand loyalty with latent dissatisfaction with SmallPhone's business performance. Max Sample is a highly commited customer of SmallPhone's, but a TRI*M performance measurement wouldn't supply an index in the top area of the scale, plus a business characteristic towards the hostage relationship typ. Max Sample's commitment has to be explained not only by performance and services he received, but also by his high involvement as well as the way he percepts brands independently from their business performance. That means: The Conversion Model segmentation focusses clearly on future behaviour by taking into account both business performance and personal attitude, whereas TRI*M provides a performance measurement together with strategic insights.

Naturally the reverse can also be the case: Low brand commitment with high satisfaction. This is the case, for example, with high involvement and only small differences in the evaluation of various competitors in the market. Customers with this profile are for example strongly price-driven consumers like Peter Price, who are very happy with their current provider, but who are always actively screening the market and will change providers without hesitation on better offers from the competition. That is, the decision on suppliers takes place exclusively following satisfaction, particularly here following price satisfaction. In this case Peter Price turns out to be, what the TRI*M Typology calls a mercenary or some marketers would call a variety seeker. In total, the outcomes in terms of the market research results would be a TRI*M Index above average, a TRI*M Typology pattern towards the mercenaries, but a commitment segmentation on the uncommitted side of the Conversion Model. Again: Whereas the Conversion Model focuses clearly on future behaviour, TRI*M provides a performance measure plus additional strategic insights.

For shampoo products, what matters for Peter Price incidentally is the opposite of the mobile phone case: The subject does not interest him, he is not involved, he considers all brands as if they were the same, all shampoos used by him up till now fulfil his (small) expectations of the product. Business performance does not play a big role for his decision for a brand. His experience that all products are the same, even deepens his low involvement in the product category. That is why time and again he decides spontaneously at the point of sale on the new shampoo product. The result is that he often buys the market leader, because of its "highest visibility", or he uses one of the colourfully advertised current special offers. This leads to a high repertoire of brands, he has used in the past. It is completely impossible to make a brand-loyal consumer out of Peter Price, just because his involvement in the product category turns out to be significantly low. Probably, one would end up with a poor commitment measure, an average performance indication and an indifferent Typology tag.

Two examples, two different specimens. Apart from segmentation after Commitment, the Conversion Model offers an ancillary tool – the so-called *States of Mind* – which illustrates precisely these connections analysed and in the form of an additional segmentation at the level of the market or the brand.

TRI*M and Conversion Model Questions

The two sets of measures validate and yet they do not correlate:

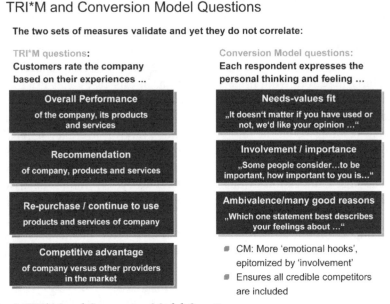

TRI*M questions:
Customers rate the company based on their experiences ...

Overall Performance
of the company, its products and services

Recommendation
of company, products and services

Re-purchase / continue to use
products and services of company

Competitive advantage
of company versus other providers in the market

Conversion Model questions:
Each respondent expresses the personal thinking and feeling ...

Needs-values fit
„It doesn't matter if you have used or not, we'd like your opinion ..."

Involvement / importance
„Some people consider...to be important, how important to you is..."

Ambivalence/many good reasons
„Which one statement best describes your feelings about ..."

- CM: More 'emotional hooks', epitomized by 'involvement'
- Ensures all credible competitors are included

Fig. 5. TRI*M and Conversion Model Questions

The most interesting segment in terms of the relevance of the business performance are the *Seekers*, whose brand commitment is primarily driven by perception of the same. These consumers are not bound to "their" brand, because they break down on fundamental performance criteria. In terms of the TNS tools, a very high connection thus exists in this segment between the TRI*M Index as a measurement of business performance and brand loyalty, hence the allocation to a Conversion Model Segment. For brand control, this means that in this particular customer segment efforts must be made, particularly with drivers of satisfaction, derived from the TRI*M Grid as a tool for the TRI*M driver analysis.

If the TRI*M analysis supplies on a total level, i.e. for all customers, a holistic evaluation of all business processes and super-ordinate starting points for their improvement, then the TRI*M Grid for the *Seeker* supplies particular starting points for those customers for whom the remaining – or rather classic – measures of brand control, like marketing and communication, do not promise resounding success. At this point the TRI*M (process) analysis and brand analysis interlink with and cross-fertilise each other: The *States of Mind* analysis delivers results in a segment that is often neglected in classic brand management because of a focus on advertising and communication, and the TRI*M analysis delivers in a very clear form and manner the particular starting points for this segment.

TRI*M Grid

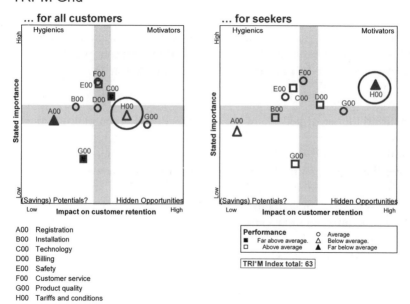

Fig. 6. TRI*M Grid

Conversely, it also becomes clear from what is said that the inclusion of brand commitment can represent an enrichment of the business performance analysis. For instance, the *States of Mind* can be used as a starting variable in the framework of a TRI*M analysis, on the one hand in order to get a better understanding of relations of cause and effect, and on the other hand to achieve an efficient allocation of resources when planning measures for improvement.

Back to our example: For SmallPhone this would mean that a combined analysis by means of the Conversion Model and TRI*M would identify Max Sample as a *"single minded customer"* to whom one must pay particular attention with appropriate communicative bonding measures, while Peter Price would be identified as a *"seeker"*, who must be permanently convinced by an above average business performance in comparison with the competition. The Seeker TRI*M Grid delivers the awareness that customers like Peter Price look in the first place for the attractiveness of tariffs. The overall TRI*M analysis ultimately identifies strengths and weaknesses in Smallphone's business performance, and thus supplies valuable starting points e.g. for quality management and customer service.

12.5 Conclusion

The fate of many articles such as this one is that often it is only the introduction and conclusion that are read. For this reason, we want at this point to come back to the original questions posed at the outset and to briefly summarise the results.

As has been demonstrated, there are overlaps between the measurement of business performance with TRI*M and the measurement of brand commitment by means of the Conversion Model. Both tools aim to improve the relationship of a business with its customers and with it the profitability of the enterprise. The perspective of both tools is different however. On the one hand are the process, service and product optimisation, implemented via a TRI*M analysis, on the other hand the strengthening of brands via an improved brand perception in the minds of the consumers, implemented via the Conversion Model. While TRI*M applies first and foremost to the analysis of the business situation and for example stands ready with the TRI*M Grid Tools to support the optimisation processes mentioned, the Conversion Model explicitly focuses on the prognosis of brand change and offers in its segmentation the appropriate tool for analysis.

The results of both tools are applicable and interpretable separately from each other; however the combination of both perspectives extends the possibilities of interpretation and the recommendations for action.

TRI*M and Conversion Model

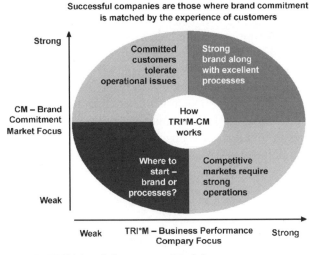

Fig. 7. TRI*M and Conversion Model

In our view, the combination of the TRI*M and Conversion Model tools adds genuine value to the analysis in practice. A substantial argument for it lies in the relatively large gain in information for relatively little outlay, as the Conversion Model can be easily integrated as an add-on into existing TRI*M studies. In content, the Conversion Model supplements the TRI*M philosophy in two basic aspects:

1. The business perspective, which is the basis of the TRI*M philosophy, is extended to the market and brand view of the Conversion Model. This makes the results of the straightforward customer survey holistically interpretable.
2. The "hard" TRI*M questions, the answers to which are based strictly on a consumer's experience, are supplemented with the "soft" questions of the Conversion Model, which take into consideration affinities and preferences. A combined research approach thus considers both the experiences and the attitudes of the consumer.

To the extent that it promises much for a stronger dovetailing of customer and brand loyalty research, the combination of both approaches can effectively contribute to the success of a business.

References

More on the Conversion Model at *www.conversionmodel.com*

13 How Does Customer Retention Work?

Apostolos Apergis

13.1 Introduction

Winning new customers is by far more difficult and expensive than keeping existing customers. This is widely known across industries. That is why companies try to understand how exactly customer relations work, what customers particularly like about their offers, what drives customers to switch to the competition, or why some customers give a large proportion of their business to one supplier and only a small proportion to others.

TNS, with its proprietary TRI*M system, is the worldwide market leader in the area of stakeholder management, i.e. the management of all relationships a company has with the parties that have a stake in the company. Customers take the primary place among stakeholders. This report summarises the most important insights from our 15 years of practical experience in customer retention research, based on over 12,000 projects.

13.2 Even Satisfied Customers Defect

Many companies regularly conduct customer surveys to measure customer satisfaction. However, it is not customer satisfaction that is decisive but rather customer retention. Satisfaction can be instrumental for customer retention, but it is not sufficient – as we have experienced in numerous projects. Even satisfied customers defect. Satisfaction without loyalty can lead to habituation and boredom. The customer is keen to experience something new and therefore changes to another supplier.

Customer relations are too complex to capture their intensity with just one dimension. TNS uses a customer retention Index, consisting of four dimensions (questions), which cover rational and emotional aspects. One dimension in this context is whether the working relations yield an advantage: Thus, we enquire how big the advantage is in working together with the present supplier rather than any other supplier.

The question on the advantage distinguishes the 'best' from the 'good' companies. Customers who perceive a big advantage with their supplier are more loyal. They compare the competition's offer less often, share their positive experiences with others, and are less price-sensitive.

13.3 Satisfied Customers Are Good; Loyal Customers Are Better

Without doubt, a company likes those customers best who are satisfied as well as loyal. But companies have strategies, i.e. they decide in favour of certain options and dismiss others. Hence, they cannot meet the needs and requirements of all customers. Should one focus on aiming at the satisfaction of only a certain percentage of the customers? Or do dissatisfied customers also provide a profitable business potential?

Consumer Typology of Industrial Companies Worldwide

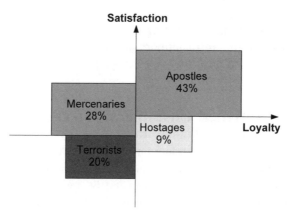

Source: TRI*M benchmarking database; based on 500.000 interviews with industrial customers, 2003-06
Typology: Jones & Sasser, Harvard Business Review Nov. 96

Fig. 1. Every Fith Customer of Industrial Companies Is Neither Satisfied nor Loyal

In order to provide well-founded answers to these questions, TNS uses the instrument of customer typology, which was developed by Harvard professors Jones and Sasser in the mid-1990s. In this typology, customers are evaluated on the dimensions of satisfaction and loyalty.

Fig. 1 depicts the customer typology of suppliers for industrial products and services worldwide. ‚Apostles' represent the ideal customers: They are satisfied and loyal. They make up a sizable 43% of customers. A further 28% are 'Mercenaries', who are also satisfied but less loyal customers. These are the customers who regularly look for the next bargain.

'Hostages' (9%) on the other hand, are for various reasons tied to the company, although they are dissatisfied. Technological dependencies, long-term contracts or logistical and regional restrictions can be the reasons as to why these customers do not change provider. Finally, 20% of the customers of industrial companies are neither satisfied nor loyal – these customers are described as 'Terrorists'.

They have had negative experiences with the products and services of their suppliers and in turn damage the image of the company by telling colleagues and business partners about it.

Having satisfied customers alone is not enough. Dissatisfied but loyal customers, namely 'Hostages' are often quite attractive. Fig. 2 depicts this correlation using the example of a specialised retailer. 'Hostages' purchase twice as frequently as 'Mercenaries' and spend more per purchase. Thus, they generate on average three times as much turnover for this specialised retailer as 'Mercenaries'.

Companies with a large proportion of 'Terrorists' must identify the causes for this. These can be found in the processes and the product offerings, i.e. the companies themselves create their own 'Terrorists': A call centre, which keeps customers waiting for too long, turns a number of callers into 'Terrorists' every day. If these customers are more effectively dealt with during the actual telephone conversation, a number of them can be won back. Consequently, the typology delivers insights about the processes of the company rather than about the customers.

Almost all companies have dissatisfied customers. But not all dissatisfied customers are identical. If, for example, a company succeeds in binding dissatisfied customers to long-term service contracts, these can turn out to be more valuable than satisfied customers.

Purchase Behaviour at a Specialised Retailer

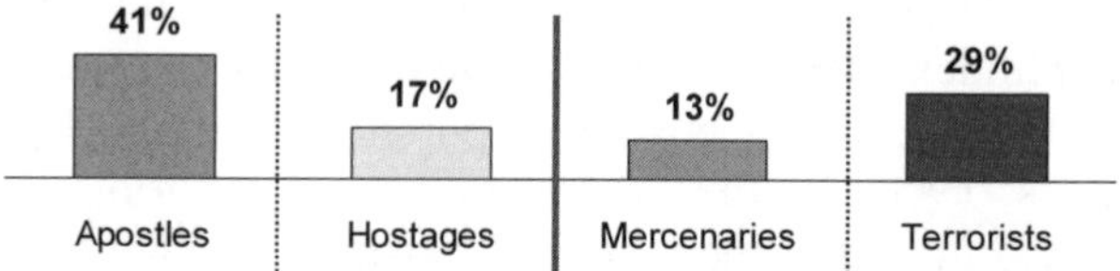

	Apostles	Hostages	Mercenaries	Terrorists
	41%	17%	13%	29%
Ø Number of Visits p.a.	31	22	11	7
Ø Turnover per Visit	$55	$43	$30	$16
Ø Turnover p.a.	$1705	$946	$330	$112

Fig. 2. 'Hostages' Are More Valuable Ccustomers than 'Mercenaries'

13.4 There Is a Correlation Between Customer Retention and Business Success – but This Varies from Business to Business

Companies are increasingly looking for a monetary justification of their customer retention measures, as they want to assure themselves that investments into customer relations pay off. According to our experience, the TRI*M customer retention Index which TNS has been measuring for companies in all industries for 15 years, is clearly related to business success. However, this correlation cannot be generalised but rather depends on the industry, the type of business, and sometimes even the customer segment.

TNS frequently has the opportunity to quantify the correlation of the TRI*M Index with the business success by means of internal company data. A project carried out a for a mobile network operator for instance, demonstrated that the churn rate of mobile network customers increases when the TRI*M Index drops. If the Index drops from 80 to 50 points, customers are twice as likely to change to a competitor within the next 12 months.

At first glance this is not surprising, but it goes to show that the Index is an early indicator for business-critical performance metrics.

A project carried out a for a corporate bank, showed that the customer retention index influenced the 'share of wallet', meaning the proportion of total services corporate customers purchase from this bank (see Fig. 3).

Customer Retention and Share of Wallet at a Corporate Bank

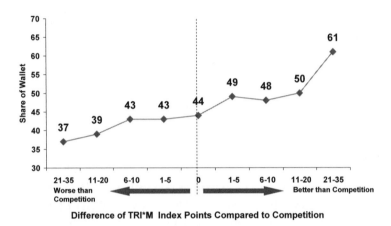

Fig. 3. The Greater the Difference of the TRI*M Index Compared with the Competition, the Greater the Share of Wallet

Most corporate customers work with two or more banks. In this project, the customers assessed their experiences with the bank and the most important competitor. The group of customers, with which the bank had an Index of more than 20 points higher than the competitor's Index, had more than 60% of their business with that bank.

In other projects TNS were able to verify the impact customer retention has on the price sensibility, the profitability, or the annual business volume with the customer. Whether the degree of customer retention influences the business success via a binary decision (customers stay with a provider or defect – as in the mobile network example) or via the intensity of transactions (many or few transactions – as in the corporate banking example) is a question with no general answer. In order to understand this correlation, companies need to analyse their customer relations more precisely and identify those factors that are crucial for customer retention.

13.5   Don't Believe Everything the Customer Tells You

Knowing the degree of customer retention is not enough. Companies also want to learn what the drivers of customer retention are and how they perform in the eyes of the customers. Every customer satisfaction survey tries to answer these questions.

TRI*M analyses the drivers for customer retention using three dimensions, which are shown on the TRI*M Grid, the core of our studies. The 'communication axis' indicates what is important to the customers and what they talk about. The 'action axis' indicates the impact on customer retention. The further right an element is situated, the stronger it drives customer retention. Finally, the symbol represents the third dimension, namely the performance of the company.

Fig. 4 shows how a technology provider was assessed by its customers with regard to order process and delivery. The surveyed customers assessed the elements "completeness of the quotation" (A1), "time schedule in the quotation meets customer requirements" (A2) and "on-time delivery" (A4) as equally important. The driver analysis of the TRI*M Grid reveals, however, that only the latter ("on-time delivery") greatly influences customer retention and is therefore a 'Motivator'. Here, there is urgent need for action as the triangle signifies a clear weakness. In other words, the company provides a complete quotation promising to meet time schedule requirements, but fails to keep this promise in the end.

Customer Assessment of a Technology Provider

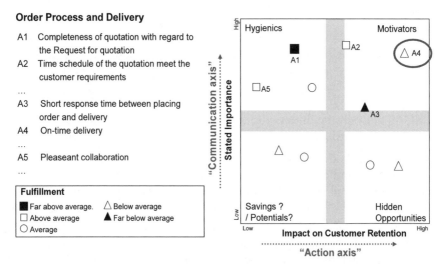

Order Process and Delivery

A1 Completeness of quotation with regard to the Request for quotation

A2 Time schedule of the quotation meet the customer requirements

...

A3 Short response time between placing order and delivery

A4 On-time delivery

...

A5 Pleaseant collaboration

...

Fulfillment

■ Far above average. △ Below average

□ Above average ▲ Far below average

○ Average

Fig. 4. First Priority Should Always Be to Remove Weaknesses in the 'Motivator' Feld

The fact that the employees are perceived as pleasant during the collaboration (A5) is only a small consolation as the influence on customer retention is low. First priority should always be to remove the triangles from the 'Motivator' field.

During TNS' 15 years of practical experience, the TRI*M Grid has proved to be an important management tool. The Grid is compact but nevertheless captures the full complexity of the customer relationship. It draws the management's attention to the top priority issues without oversimplifying the results. In other words, the TRI*M Grid is a kind of x-ray of the customer relationship. Managing directors in all industries use the TRI*M Grid to understand the numerous facets of their customer relationships, derive measures and manage the strategic alignment of the company.

13.6 Understanding How Customer Retention Works Not Only Provides Insights About the Customers, but also About the Company

Companies usually conduct customer surveys to learn more about customers' expectations and needs. In addition to this, TRI*M users receive further insights about their own customer interfaces and processes.

At the end of the 1990s, a new mobile network company had a roaming agreement with the incumbent operator in order to provide nation-wide coverage while its own network infrastructure was being setup in rural areas.

At the end of the 1990s, a new mobile network company had a roaming agreement with the incumbent operator in order to provide nation-wide coverage while its own network infrastructure was being setup in rural areas.

The management decided to stop this cost-intensive agreement for one region when its own infrastructure there appeared to be sufficiently setup. All internal indicators supported this decision. However, the TRI*M Index, measured in the weeks after the roaming agreement ended, indicated that the segment of 'very mobile heavy users' were experiencing now a deterioration in the network quality. Reception broke up regularly while travelling in and out of the affected region because the company's own infrastructure proved to be less stable than anticipated. The insights gained from this customer survey convinced the management to reconsider their decision and to plan future switch to the company's network more carefully.

Another example comes from an IT infrastructure-provider, facing considerable difficulties in implementing cross-selling for a major key account. The management commissioned a TRI*M study to analyse the customer relationship. The assessment of project managers and the account manager supplied particularly conclusive insights. Although both were available on-site at the customer's location and understood his business requirements, they were not proactive and were restricted in their ability to make decisions. A subsequent workshop showed that these issues were caused by an unclear allocation of responsibilities within the sales organisation. Based upon these results, the management revised the customer interface and re-organised the team of managers.

If a company plans to realign its processes and organisation, the customers' viewpoint should always be taken into consideration.

13.7 The Drivers for Customer Retention Vary over the Course of Time

Companies innovate their products and processes to gain advantages over the competition. Over the course of time however, most innovations are copied and become a standard that is taken for granted. UPS created a competitive advantage when, in 1993, it introduced "track-and trace", an innovation soon copied by other courier services. Fig. 5 shows the course that "track-and-trace" took on the TRI*M Grid. At first, it appeared as a possible 'Potential or Saving', and then, in 1995, moved into the field of 'Hidden Opportunities'. In 2000, it changed into a clear 'Motivator', and later moved to the left, to become a classic 'Hygienic factor': Today, every courier offers "track-and-trace", be it over the telephone or online and customers take this for granted. Therefore, this element is no longer a driver for customer retention.

Innovations that start in the field of 'Savings? / Potentials?', as was the case with "track-and-trace", should be closely monitored. They often move over the course of time to the right, and become Hidden Opportunities. Three years ago, a service-provider for electricity network operators introduced analysis of cost effectiveness for network components as an offering. In the beginning, customers perceived this offering as irrelevant. Today, this offering is a Hidden Opportunity: Most customers don't demand this service – but those who ordered it were able to save operating costs and will continue to work with this provider in the future. The service-provider should now further improve its performance and communicate more strongly about it. If the offering of cost-effectiveness analysis turns into a 'Motivator' in future, the company would then gain a competitive advantage. Therefore, the field of Hidden Opportunities yields sources for tomorrow's competitive advantage.

172

Track and Trace in the Courier Service Industry:
Change over the Course of Time

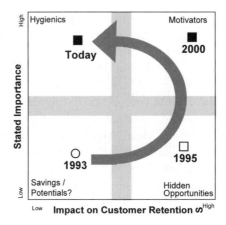

Fig. 5. "Track-and-trace": From 'Innovation' to 'Competitive Advantage' to "Industry Standard'

13.8   In Order to Align the Organisation with Customer Requirements, Actions and Measurable Targets Are Essential

A TRI*M study into customer retention supplies an excellent basis for deducing customer-related objectives for management. As mentioned before, the TRI*M Index is related to financial performance indicators such as share of wallet and profitability, and thus is relevant for economic success.

Furthermore, the Index is so stable that even a change of three points can only be achieved with considerable effort.

Finally, the TRI*M Grid provides insights for increasing customer retention. In an implementation workshop, which is often facilitated by TNS consultants, causes are analysed, and suggestions for measures are developed. As important as the customers' point of view may be, only company executives have an overview of all relevant influence-factors and are responsible for the selection of measures to improve customer retention. It is crucial that the measures are embedded in the overall strategy. This way, TRI*M supports the decision-making process of management.

In numerous companies, the TRI*M customer-retention Index is used as a component for employees' target agreements. A part of variable remuneration of managers is often linked to the Index. Companies have various options to put this into practice. There are three basic variants:

1) A company-wide Index, which influences the performance-related salary component of all employees

2) Separate Indices for every business unit with profit/loss-responsibility (e.g. region, division, customer segment, or individual key accounts)

3) Indices alongside the value chain, i.e. for the individual functions (e.g. sales, customer care, technical service). Here, the individual elements from the TRI*M Grid are bundled into a functional Index relevant to employees in these functions. At the same time the overall TRI*M Index on the level of the business unit can be used as an optional further component influencing the variable pay.

Which option a company decides to apply depends mainly on the company strategy and the customer interface: A plant manufacturer links the customer-retention Index of individual key accounts with the target agreement of the respective account teams. A retail bank relates the bonus for its employees to the regional Index, which includes several branches, but provides its employees with TRI*M Grids and reports on branch-level. Finally, a telecommunications provider, whose strategic goal is to improve its customer service, uses only the national overall Index for the variable remuneration of all its employees.

13.9 Customer Retention Management Is a Part of Stakeholder Management

Stakeholder management is the management of all the relationships a company has with the parties that have a stake in the company. Customers are primary stakeholders, with employees, investors and business partners also being important parties. In this context, customer retention management is part of stakeholder management. The TRI*M system can be extended to the management of all stakeholders. In addition to its use for assessing customer retention, numerous companies apply TRI*M to manage employee commitment and internal service quality. By simultaneously implementing these stakeholder management systems, companies increase the value-add of the results and obtain a holistic information basis for making decisions (integrated approach).

14 Implementing the TRI*M Approach as a Stakeholder Management System for Russia's Largest Telecom Provider

Simon Priadko

The VimpelCom Group is one of the largest telecom providers in the Russian and former CIS countries markets. The VimpelCom Group includes companies operating in Russia, Kazakhstan, Ukraine, Uzbekistan, Tajikistan, Georgia and Armenia. The VimpelCom Group's GSM and 3G license portfolio covers a territory with a population of about 250 million. This includes the entire territories of Russia, Kazakhstan, Ukraine, Uzbekistan, Tajikistan, Georgia and Armenia. VimpelCom was the first Russian company to list its shares on the New York Stock Exchange ("NYSE"). VimpelCom's ADSs are listed on the NYSE under the symbol "VIP".

TRI*M has been systematically applied at Vimpelcom for a couple of years, first of all as a Customer Retention and more broadly speaking as a "Brand Health" Tool.

Thanks to the personal involvement of Dr. Joachim Scharioth, who personally introduced and explained TRI*M at Vimpelcom and supported the rollout from a distance, and across the local TNS team, the TRI*M system was successfully implemented and is now regarded as a flexible research tool for Customer Retention Management.

It is worth noting that the understanding of the vital importance of Human Resources and the acceptance of implementing Customer Retention instruments in developing markets is still a rare case, and Russia is not an exception in this matter (a white crow as they say).

The earlier a company realizes that Customer Retention is inevitable the better it is for business. The already saturated mobile market confronts the companies with the challenge of securing loyalty and increased retention instead of purely focusing on customer acquisition. Needless to say, investments to make consumers switch their telecom provider are higher than those of keeping loyal and existing ones. Therefore, the idea is not having simply a research technique, but a business tool to plan and monitor investments effectively in line with the company's chosen strategy.

As one of the first in the country Vimpelcom started gradually with the monitoring of their TRI*M Index in 2004.

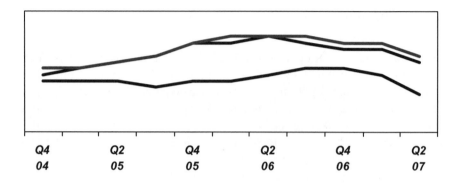

*Fig. 1. TRI*M Index over Time for Key Market Players in Russia*

It is shown above that the more saturated the market is, the more difficult it is to keep the Retention Index high, as subscribers become more knowledgeable and also have higher demands and expectations. We observe the stabilization of the Index with the trend for a decline for all key market players in Russia.

Quickly enough the management developed a more challenging task to adapt the system to their business, and it became evident that the TRI*M Index had to be supplemented by touch points measurement (so-called bundles). To reach this goal, several separate research projects were conducted (qualitative and quantitative), and a number of bundles were singled out, such as: Network, Products, Sales Channels, Service, etc, which are important for clients in certain areas for which they vote with their money when choosing the brand. Thus, various business units of the company responsible for the selected touch points received a transparent and manageable business monitoring tool, under the umbrella of a simple KPI (Key Performance Indicator) system.

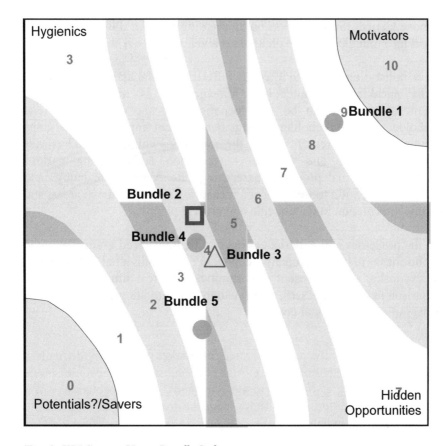

Fig. 2. KPI System Using Bundle Indices

The tool has been built into a strategic monitoring system, which measures the "business temperature" at least twice a year, very comparable with the health check recommended to each individual by doctors.

Each of the bundles is further broken down into their specific parameters using the TRI*M Grid, and is monitored as well to get the understanding of the reasons for performance of the bundle index at the higher level.

Naturally, a gap appears between strategic and operational monitoring. For the latter, various instruments are used, which assist to easily and quickly fine tune the performance of each touch point, if an alarm signal is received. To name just a few, those can be separated into complaint management systems from the clients (various hotlines, etc), and external research techniques (various satisfaction measurements, etc).

All those tactical tools function on an ongoing basis in the company, and support the strategic tool, but on a micro level.

Such a holistic approach to Customer Retention Management and more broadly speaking – Stakeholder Management, is not new, but if implemented wisely can be very beneficial for the company and its shareholders. The Stakeholder Management System implies a wider scope of temperature measurements inside the company – employee and business processes research, and outside – reputation audit among various stakeholders, external processes assessment, etc. Vimpelcom enjoys and pays special attention to this concept, measuring all of the above areas, and uses this information in its strategic and tactical planning.

Now the processes and experiences have to be transferred gradually to the CIS business of the company, depending on individual geographies business tasks, which present opportunities for great multi-cultural and comparison across businesses, which cannot but provide great assets to the business of a multinational company.

15   A Framework for Social Development Assessment[*]

Daniel Lindgren, John Budd

15.1   The Behavioural Change Challenge

Behavioural change is probably the single most difficult objective communicators are asked to undertake. In the private sector it is an area which falls under marketing, and in the context of development it could also be called social marketing. Nor is behavioural change communication confined to the developing world. Countries at all levels of development undertake mass awareness campaigns in order to influence behaviours, as does the private sector.

In the private sector a huge research industry has developed to provide consumer insights and answers about behaviours. It is the same in the development context. Consumer research is called KAP surveys – knowledge, attitude and practice. But such research is often narrowly focused and too often a one-way street. Impact studies are conducted but mainly to inform communicators about the effectiveness of their specific campaigns and messages. How beneficiaries regard the campaign and the issue as a whole and what they think is beneficial or even needed in the broader context of the services provided is often overlooked. So the question is, how can we use the beneficiary's perceptions of the effectiveness of a campaign in order for it to be more effective? In other words start a dialogue – make the beneficiary an active participant in the process.

In Indonesia, UNICEF stumbled into this accidentally when ensuring that efforts in the reconstruction of tsunami ravaged Aceh were effective and being well received by the beneficiaries, and could be reported to donors around the world. Having successfully conducted research in 2004-2005 and then in 2005-2006, it was decided to apply the same framework to

[*] This article was first published in Public Opinion Polling in a Globalized World, Carballo, Marita; Hjelmar, Ulf (Eds.), © 2008 Springer

assess public awareness campaigns UNICEF was conducting on avian influenza in 2006-2007.

15.2 An Idea Was Formed

Looking at the social research scene in Indonesia, most work that TNS and other international research agencies carry out is with large aid and donor organizations or through consultancies servicing these clients in a broader context. Polling through media remains under developed or is served by local agencies on a much smaller scale. The same applies to government work and means revenue streams from these alternative sources remains very limited. But then again, Indonesia, the world's largest archipelago as well as the most populous Muslim nation, presents plenty of work opportunities for donor organizations.

Working closely with several of the world's most prominent aid and donor agencies, one of the main challenges that is evident is the need for good program evaluations. Aid organizations in particular, large and small, receive a large proportion of their funding for specific projects. As with any commercial operator aid organizations often have to compete for this, often limited, pool of funds. There is a tender process and the aid organization has to present a strong case for their project in terms of how it will contribute to the betterment for beneficiaries as well as how results will be evaluated. Donors, like investors, would reasonable like to know that the money was well spent. Hence, some, but far from all, social development projects have a research component for evaluation. Ideally there should be a baseline measure followed by an impact measure. But more often than expected perhaps, the evaluation is conducted internally in sometimes very ambiguous and arbitrary circumstances. Audits are part of daily life in commercial operations (Scharioth, Huber 2003). But anyone dealing with large aid organizations will be aware of the frantic atmosphere in the client's office at the end of a large project. Yes, the auditors are coming and everyone is scrambling to come up with a good story to show that their contribution was indeed worth while. Having met with many program staff across an array of different organizations it is amazing to see their commitment to their work. Not to mention the field operators, who are often tucked away in the bush somewhere without access to modest, or even basic, conveniences. Their inspiration stems from caring about people in need and because they themselves believe a difference can be made.

At the end of the day it would often be unfair to question their commitment to the cause, but donors want proof of their work in terms of measurable outcomes. Key Performance Indicators or KPIs is a term with which aid organizations are quickly becoming more familiar. Aid organizations are slowly beginning to realize that even the *warm and fuzzy* world of social development is becoming subject to accountability. No doubt many resist this but there seems to be no escape.

It has been said that *what is not measured cannot be managed*. How true it is and perhaps one could argue that common sense also dictates this. But it has also been said that *common sense is not common*. In the case of social development work what one has to remember is that these are no ordinary projects, it is very complex often involving multiple organizations seeking to assist beneficiaries from impoverished, difficult to reach regions under adverse circumstances. From a research perspective, measurement becomes a daunting task both in terms of sampling as well as developing suitable survey instruments.

15.3 Developing a Social Assessment Framework

Stakeholder Management is an area of expertise within TNS and those working in this field have a number of models and tools to their disposal. The question was whether appraisal of social development work can be viewed as a stakeholder management problem? Secondly, would it be possible to apply one of TNS's more popular models called TRI*M? The power of the TRI*M model is not so much in it's statistical rigor, nor the fact that it has been subjected to numerous validations across all sorts of markets and industries (Huber, Scharioth, Pallas 2004). No, the attractiveness really lies in its flexibility and being able to strike a cord with clients in the most varied of circumstances. Still, the area of social development research seemed like a tough challenge but still possible, somehow.

At the outset of developing the social assessment framework, the vision was clear. The framework should help to identify specific focal points that can help aid and donor organizations to achieve enhanced results.

From a client perspective, the following benefits were seen to be relevant:

- To have the ability to map stakeholder needs geographically
- To focus on specific beneficiaries or stakeholder groups, in a more relevant way
- To be able to prioritize program initiatives and activities
- To assess the deployment of resources & effort
- To benchmark performance across activity areas

In order to deliver on those benefits, the social assessment framework itself must adhere to some basic guidelines. This was necessary to ensure the framework can be adopted in a local as well as global context.

- Provide for a consistent format across: Time, communities / regions, programs, participating organizations
- Accessible & easily comparable understanding to facilitate learning and dissemination of results
- Build pro-active thinking in the form of a red-flag or early warning mechanism
- High level insight for strategy development down to specific task related information for program management

But how is social development work related to corporate reputation? As has been pointed out, the truth is that many aid and donor organizations are not able to effectively measure the performance of social development programs. Within the area of corporate reputation, effective tools have been developed over the years to allow organizations to becoming more knowledgeable about their own industry (O'Gorman, Pirner, 2006). Understanding ones corporate reputation provides for a holistic picture of how different stakeholder groups view an organization as well as how the company should align its resources to communicate more effectively (Hermann 2007). It is all about building awareness, changing attitudes, and ultimately have people behave is such a way that it benefits the company.

The same applies to social development work, which in most part is about making people aware and changing the way they think and behave.

Looking at the stakeholders themselves beneficiaries are at the core, rather than customers. And just as corporate reputation is dependent on several stakeholder groups, social development programs rely on support from multiple parties often including various government departments.

Looking at the stakeholders themselves beneficiaries are at the core, rather than customers. And just as corporate reputation is dependent on several stakeholder groups, social development programs rely on support from multiple parties often including various government departments.

Communication is not about selling a product or service but rather to inform and educate as an end goal (selling ideas). Whether in a commercial or social context, media spending can be substantial and media channels employed can be similar. It is sometimes necessary to develop peoples' mind-sets by changing their attitudes. Just a like a mining company wants people to be forgiving towards its impact on the environment, a social development program on AIDS wants people to acknowledge there are people who live with this decease and they should not be ignored. Ultimately and ideally, social change is about engagement through participation rather than persuasion. But the ultimate goal of a social development program is not to build a reputation for the organization behind the program but rather for the program itself.

15.4   Program Effectiveness Index

The first basic building block of the social assessment framework is the Program Effectiveness Index (PEI). The idea behind the index is to capture the relevant elements that help to determine perceived effectiveness of a social development program. The table below shows the original TRI*M index dimensions for corporate reputation together with the modified dimensions for program effectiveness.

Corporate Reputation	Program Effectiveness
Overall reputation	Extent of effort behind the program
Emotional Appeal	Emotional engagement
Favourability towards the organization	Favourability towards the program
Trust in the organization	Trust in what is being communicated
Competence	Effective engagement
Financial or economic success	Success of the program to convince people to take action
Products & service quality	Quality of program communication

*Fig. 1. TRI*M Index Dimensions*

The relevance behind each of the index dimensions can be highlighted with a simple example. The Avian Influenza that first appeared in Indonesia in early 2006 has been subject to a lot of attention globally. A collaborative effort is currently in place to inform the public in Indonesia about its risks, how to avoid contracting the virus, and how to prevent it from spreading further. First of all, are people aware and do they see a concerted effort behind the Avian Influenza program? This does not only involve UNICEF and the government of Indonesia but several other organisations, all working to combat the threat of a possible pandemic. Secondly, are people emotionally engaged? In other words, do they support the program and do they feel that what is being communicated is relevant and make sense? Finally, there needs to be a link to behavioural change through effective engagement. So, is there a sense that the Avian Influenza program is working in terms of changing behaviour and is communication of good quality?

Having a standardised, independently measured PEI has an important advantage in that it can be used across countries and programs. This allows for effective benchmarking, a tool which is becoming more and more essential for global companies including aid and donor organisations. Further, the PEI allows for flexibility in terms of diagnosing the level of performance across time, geographical areas, stakeholder groups, and time. So it is a very effective monitoring tool and provides for a quick overview of where a particular program is working and where it is having less impact.

15.5   Case Study – Aceh Tsunami Relief

The 2004 Tsunami disaster was an event that captured the attention of the entire globe. Indonesia had the biggest death toll with some quarter of a million people confirmed dead or missing. No less than 385,256 people were displaced, loosing their home, family members or both (UN Information Management Service 2005). The table below shows some of the worse hit regions. The 8.6 magnitude earthquake on the island of Nias, that struck shortly after the Tsunami made matters worse. The disaster was met by unprecedented support from the international community and it has been estimated that some 200 organizations set up base in Aceh alone to assist in the relief effort. The amount of donations contributed from the international community was so significant that it far exceeded what is needed for the reconstruction effort. Yet, the traumatized region is still struggling to get back on its feet.

This may seem odd but the fact is, having excess funds only adds to the problem, especially in Indonesia, one of the world's most notorious nations for corruption. Too much money brings out the worst in people and means the relief effort has in many parts been brought down on its knees with very little progress, especially in the first 12 months (TNS Indonesia 2006). Having so many organizations operating simultaneously adds to the complexity and coordination alone has become a gigantic task.

Regions Hit by Tsunami	Internally Displaced Persons (IDPs)
Aceh Besar	45,269
Nias	30,307
Aceh Barat	25,137
Aceh Jaya	22,306
Banda Aceh	19,944
Pidie	19,279
Nias Selatan	11,893
Total	**174,135**

Fig. 2. Tsunami Figures in Indonesia

Amongst other organizations operating in Aceh and Nias, UNICEF is playing a key role in the rebuilding of the disaster struck area. Focusing on the areas of health, education, water & sanitation and child protection, UNICEF has a fair challenge in coordinating its own activities. Research carried out by TNS in 2005 confirmed the notion that the relief effort, whilst moving in the right direction, was not moving ahead quickly enough. Feedback from beneficiaries was therefore needed to understand their perceptions as to how effective the relief effort has been. The brief from UNICEF was simple, what are the red button issues that IDPs want to see improved immediately? With this brief, the first opportunity to test the new social assessment framework had materialized.

The performance effectiveness index was able to show that performance varied across regions. The index showed that the more easily reached regions, Banda Aceh and Aceh Besar, had the worst performance ratings whereas Aceh Barat and Aceh Jaya, some of the most badly hit remote regions, had significantly better performance ratings. However, when sharing the results with UNICEF staff in the respective regions said they were not surprised. Banda Aceh as the capital of the province has served as a hub for much of the relief effort. IDPs in this area have had relatively easy access to assistance without having to rely on their own efforts.

186

Whilst the devastation was large, many parts of Banda Aceh and Aceh Besar were unaffected and meant IDPs were not totally stranded. This led to IDPs becoming somewhat complacent. In contrast, more remote regions have had relatively limited resources to begin with and meant that IDPs and their local communities had to put in significant effort to rebuild their lives, to survive. This logic became evident when looking at the extent to which IDPs have developed a *mind-set* that was coherent with the program objectives outlined by UNICEF. In short, an examination was done in relation to IDPs knowledge, attitude and behaviour to see how developed their mind-set was in order to cope and improve their livelihood.

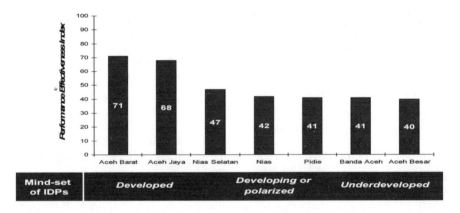

Fig. 3. Performance Effectiveness Index

Figure 3 clearly shows that IDPs in Banda Aceh and Aceh Besar had a much less developed mind-set compared to Aceh Barat and Aceh Jaya. In other words, there was a very strong association between program performance and the actual ability of IDPs to cope and improve their livelihood.

Apart from understanding performance across regions, UNICEF wanted to understand what activities were actually driving program performance. This brings us to the second part of the social assessment framework, the TRI*M Grid. In addition to the PEI, a number of specific performance attributes (e.g. program activities, communication channels, etc) are independently measured. In order to uncover the more important attributes in the minds of beneficiaries, one need to go beyond what is simply stated as being important, by making a distinction between *must have* factors and those that truly drive program performance. The Grid used for this analysis has three dimensions as shown in the diagram below.

The first two dimensions include claimed importance of program attributes and perceived performance by the program to deliver on the same attributes. The third dimension looks at the impact each attribute has on the PEI. The position of the attributes on the Grid helps to understand the relevance of each activity in the minds of IDPs.

- **1. Stated importance of attributes**
  Importance on a given attribute is defined on the basis of how important it is rated in relation to all other attributes. As such, there will always be relatively important and relatively unimportant aspects to consider.

- **2. Perceived performance on each attribute**
  Performance on a given attribute is defined on the basis of how it is rated in relation to all other attributes assessed in the questionnaire. As such, there will always be relative strengths and relative weaknesses.

- **3. Impact that attributes have on the PEI**
  This is the calculated correlation between the individual attribute and the program effectiveness index. Strong correlation means the attribute will have relatively more impact on perceived performance as a whole.

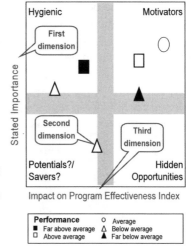

Fig. 4. Importance of Program's Attributes and Perceived Performance

Based on the three dimensions in the Grid, attributes can be classified into four groups depending on their location within the Grid (i.e. Motivators, Hygienic, Hidden Opportunities and Potential/Savers). The position on the Grid determines the relevance of each attribute. The *Motivator* quadrant is the area to observe most closely as any activity within this area is seen by beneficiaries to be a key driver for program effectiveness. *Hygienics,* on the other hand, are activities that IDPs expect to see and could relate to basic survival needs. *Hidden Opportunities* represent activities that can make a difference even though the IDPs themselves don't regard them as overly important. Finally, the *Potential/Savers* quadrant highlights activities that according to IDPs are at the bottom of the priority list. Attributes in this quadrant should be assessed in terms of being essential to the program and sometimes further education of beneficiaries is necessary.

188

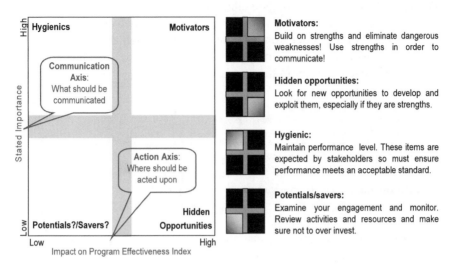

Fig. 5. Level of Relevance of Each Attribute

Looking at the 6 core program components it can be seen that UNICEF is perceived to perform well in the areas of Education and Health & Nutrition. The PEI for these activities is higher than the overall PEI of 49. The remaining program areas have a PEI lower than the average. It is interesting to note that child protection is generally not seen to be important by IDPs. Nor does it have any significant impact on program effectiveness. It is likely that more education is needed in this area and improved access to information is needed to achieve this effectively. For each program component a leverage score has been calculated which can range from 0-10. Leverage scores help to identify which program activities have the highest impact on program effectiveness, and therefore indicate the relevance for taking action. The leverage metric is intended to provide decisional support regarding resource allocation to different programs. Both Education and Health & Nutrition generate high leverage for UNICEF probably because these activities are the most visible for IDPs. On the other hand, Water & Sanitation represents a fundamental, basic need not currently met. This area became the single most important opportunity for improvement. It is also clear that the local Government in Aceh, the most important collaboration partner for UNICEF, may not be pulling their fair share of the work.

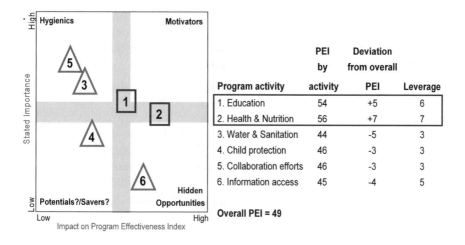

Program activity	PEI by activity	Deviation from overall PEI	Leverage
1. Education	54	+5	6
2. Health & Nutrition	56	+7	7
3. Water & Sanitation	44	-5	3
4. Child protection	46	-3	3
5. Collaboration efforts	46	-3	3
6. Information access	45	-4	5

Overall PEI = 49

Fig. 6. Table Overall Performance of Programs Activities

15.6   UNICEF View on Outcome

The development sector is a fragmented and complex beast, even within organizations. From the perspective of a communicator targeting both beneficiaries and donors, the research is an independent, valuable and measurable indicator of how work was perceived in Aceh. However the research was a little of a surprise for program staff and Government counterparts who by and large had never been subjected to beneficiary assessments of their effectiveness. They did grasp the survey's importance and at this point are still digesting the points made. It is a work in progress.

But perhaps the most important perspective on the research was UNICEF's decision in Indonesia to take it further. The looming global catastrophe of an influenza pandemic was the motivating force – and Indonesia was bird flu central. Avian influenza (H5N1) is one of the very few examples of a development issue which affects everyone, no matter where we are – bird flu doesn't stop at borders, and it pays no regard to where you come from – poor country or rich country. So what people think about bird flu in the remote distant islands of Indonesia is going to directly affect us all no matter where we are because the odds are that it will be in Indonesia or another Asia country that the virus could mutate.

It is globalization by the most unwelcome of definitions. It links the donor to the beneficiary in a challenge which will leave neither untouched.

If the governments and agencies involved in combating AI in Indonesia, or Thailand, Vietnam or China succeed it will save lives everywhere. This thought motivated the Japanese Government to provide a staggering USD 40 million grant to UNICEF to conduct a global public awareness campaign to prevent a pandemic in 2006. About USD 3.5 million was allocated to Indonesia.

The challenge was enormous. The poultry industry is massive and pre industrial. About 1.2 billion poultry in 17,000 islands spread across three time zones. Eighty percent of Indonesians raise poultry in their own backyard in a free range environment. It is an essential economic and nutrition issue for these people. Little wonder that AI was endemic throughout the country.

Fig. 7. Outbreaks Among Poultry (in Red)

From UNICEF's perspective it was also an issue killing young people and children, as looking after chickens was a chore for them.

In early 2006 we were faced with almost universal ignorance and a complete black hole of reliable, usable information about the disease. Take this from early formative research undertaken in Indonesia by USAID (USAID 2006).

"I've heard about bird flu from the media"
"To be honest, I do not really understand about bird flu"
"It only happens on TV"
"Our community isn't too concerned about AI"

Under enormous pressure to do something, anything to improve public awareness the research from USAID was used to prepared a national mass media campaign. It was hurried and not ideal because it was not possible to obtain answers to a million questions about the issue. TNS was contracted to conduct a fast and focused survey of beneficiaries in September, 2006 as the mass media campaign was starting. That research confirmed that the USAID research was accurate and that the campaign was succeeding in providing four key prevention messages, cook, separate, report and wash.

Public Service Announcement (PSA)	Effective Reach (%)
Cook	63
Separate	69
Report	44
Wash	25

Fig. 8. Program Effectiveness on Prevention Messages

The above figures are a percentage of the 500 people surveyed answering a question about whether they had seen an AI prevention message on television (TNS 2006). As you can see the survey clearly reflects the mass media messages being disseminated. The first two were PSAs already being aired prior to and during the survey period. The third advertisement had been broadcast for about a week and the fourth had just started to be shown. The mass media campaign reached well over 100 million people and ran in two blocks, September/October 2006 and February/March 2007.

All fairly crude but combined with social mobilization and advocacy campaigns in high risk areas everyone felt quietly confident that prevention information was out there and that it had reversed the overwhelming ignorance on the issue. But could any changes in behaviour be seen? Yes, in terms of institutional change. The Indonesian Government at all levels was focused on the issue but what of the individual? TNS was commissioned to conduct an impact survey using the newly developed methods presented here. The results confirmed what everyone on the campaign instinctively understood.

The survey stated that:

> Overall the AI initiative has come off to a relative good start. The perception about the initiative so far is much better compared to the Tsunami Relief Effort in Aceh for example. However, regional differences do exist and there is a strong indication that the effort is not really generating changes in behaviour, especially in rural areas where also exposure to poultry is much higher. South Sulawesi, Yogyakarta and the Botabek area are critical regions to look at to see how the AI campaign can generate more impact. This applies to both urban and rural areas (TNS 2007).

The worrying area for UNICEF was communication to people living in rural areas. Clearly there was success in providing information through national TV PSA campaigns. But, beneficiaries in the higher risk provinces of Java and South Sulawesi judged the community level/grassroots communication to need further work, especially in terms of government and community involvement. Also, resistance was anticipated based on economic imperatives overriding preventive messages, and this was again apparent in the beneficiary response.

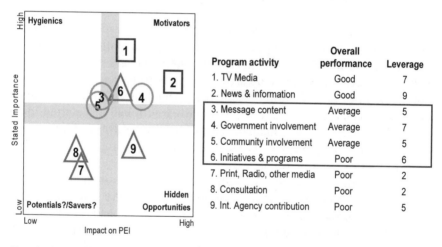

Fig. 9. Overall Performance of Program Activities in Rural Areas

But by using the leverage column it is relatively easy to see that major work should be done to obtain further government involvement. This probably has a lot to do with the traditional relationships between Indonesian people and the Government. So part of the strategy for 2007 will be to support the government in establishing district level task forces on avian influenza and piloting a range of preventative measures in a village to see what initiatives will work.

The TNS beneficiary research clearly points to a need for an adjustment in tactics, messages and targets for the remainder of the campaign in 2007-2008.

15.7 Future Perspectives

There seems to be a great interest for a tool to monitor social programs at this point in time, the time of globalization. SARS, avian Influenza and terrorism are all examples of issues that affect people across borders creating a situation in which the developed and the developing world intersect. This in turn has opened up a two-way link between beneficiaries and donors. It is no longer a situation where donors passively donate funds to a cause in a far away country. The country may still be far away but the problem may be as much their problem as the beneficiaries. For example, whilst having the largest number of confirmed deaths, the avian influenza problem is not just an Indonesia problem, it is a global problem. Hence, donors no longer want to just feel good about contributing to a good cause, they now also want to see results.

Already, the framework has established itself as a valuable monitoring and evaluating tool. It is the only independent method of assessing beneficiary attitudes to services being provided to them. But the tool should not be confined to development issues. Governments and social service providers in the developed world can use this Framework as a way of assessing their effectiveness and judging what people think is important.

The Framework was extremely helpful for UNICEF's communication outputs. The other benefit is that it provides information at two levels. The model is a bit like an iceberg, the tip is the TRI*M Index which is accessible and allows you to quickly see the most valuable insights, and beneath the surface is a wealth of supporting detailed information.

Indonesia is a country that has learnt to cope with the most testing of times. In the past 3 years it has suffered repeated natural disasters and also health crises. The Framework worked in providing the information we needed in that environment but among people who are more used to coping than others. The next step for the model is to be tested in different cultures and looking at other social issues in a less extreme situation.

Perhaps a challenge for the social development assessment framework can be put forward. Can it be used to provide vital clues as to why some of the Millennium Development Goals are being met in many regions of theworld and not in others? What do beneficiaries, the poor or the vulnerable think of this extraordinarily ambitious promise to them? Changing their perceptions, influencing their attitudes to change negative or ignorant actions into positive behaviour is one of the main means by which cycles of poverty and high risk activities can be broken. The Framework has the potential to contribute to this process. Time is running out before the deadline has to be met, but it is not too late to try out a new approach.

References

Hermann S. P, (2007) "Measuring, Managing and Monitoring CSR as a Driver for Corporate Reputation", World Council for Corporate Governance Conference-, Vilamoura, Portugal, February, 2007

Huber M, Scharioth J, Pallas M (2004), Putting Stakeholder Management into Practice, Berlin/Heidelberg: Springer

O'Gorman S, Pirner P, Measuring and monitoring Stakeholder Relationships: Suing TRI*M as an Innovative Tool for Corporate Communication, in: Huber M, Pallas M (eds.) (2006), Customising Stakeholder Management Strategies, Munich: Springer, pp 89-100

Scharioth J, Norma B, Auditing firms today and tomorrow, in: Huber M, Scharioth J, (2003), Achieving Excellence in Stakeholder Management, Berlin/Heidelberg: Springer, pp 125-140

The Millennium Development Goals Report, July, 2007

TNS Indonesia, Avian Influenza Campaign Measurement, November, 2006

TNS Indonesia, Social Development Assessment Framework: Evaluating the Performance of the National AI Initiative from a Beneficiary Perspective, May, 2007

TNS Indonesia (2006), Tsunami Relief Impact Study

UN Management Information Service in collaboration with Rehabilitation and Reconstruction Agency (BRR) (8 Dec 2005), The Tsunami Recovery Status Report

USAID, Avian Influenza: A Qualitative Research Report, May, 2006

WHO, Health Status Statistics: Mortality: Under-five and infant mortality rates, by WHO Region, 2003

Authors

Apostolos Apergis is a Director in Industrial Products and Services at TNS Infratest GmbH. During the past 12 years he has conducted projects as a market researcher and management consultant in the area of capital goods, technology and industrial services. His primary focus is on client management, distribution strategy and organisation as well as pricing.

Chapter 13

Mirko Arend, Messe München GmbH, worked at GFK Nuremberg in the B2B Market Research as well as a division manager in Market Research and Business Planning at DHL Worldwide. In 2001 he took a position at PACT, a promotions agency as their division manager in Munich. He joined Messe München GmbH in 2005 and holds his current position as a division manager and project group leader New Business Development since early 2007.

Chapter 7

Rosemary Bayman is Head of Stakeholder Management at TNS UK. After five years spent in the Financial & Professional Services division, Rosemary is now devoted to Stakeholder Management research across all industry sectors. With a focus on the customer experience, this also involves working in other stakeholder areas such as employee commitment, internal service quality and corporate reputation. She provides client consultancy, executive team advice and training in this arena across the TNS UK Custom business.

Chapter 6

John Budd, UNICEF, is a journalist by trade and inclination. For most of his 30 year career he worked for the Australian Broadcasting Corporation. He is an award winning executive producer of Australia's longest running documentary length current affairs program Four Corners, and was National Editor of TV News. After leaving the ABC he joined UNICEF in Jakarta as Head of Communication and Private Sector Fund Raising in 2003. He was part of the UNICEF team which responded to the 2004 Boxing Day tsunami in Aceh.

Chapter 15

Dr. Steffen Hermann is a Senior Consultant for Stakeholder Management at TNS Infratest GmbH. He has a shared responsibility for Hotline Consultancy at the Global TRI*M Centre and has led projects for national and international clients in different industries. His key focuses are currently Corporate Reputation / CSR and Stakeholder Management in the Consumer industry. He worked as research assistant and assistant lecturer at the private business school (HHL) of Leipzig. Steffen holds a degree in business administration and PhD specialising in marketing management.

Chapter 5

Pavel Holka, Vodafone Czech Republic, worked at GfK Praha as a research analyst following military service and graduation from university. From 2003 until mid 2007 he worked at Nestlé, initially as a market-research manager and then as the head of the Consumer & Shopper Insight team responsible for the Czech and Slovak markets. He left Nestlé in June 2007 and now works as a marketing manager at Vodafone, where he is responsible for the Market & Competitive Intelligence team.

Chapter 2

Dr. Margit Huber is Managing Director Stakeholder Management and is in charge of TNS' Area of Expertise for Stakeholder Management. She has been working at TNS since 2000 on projects in the area of Customer Satisfaction, Employee Commitment and Internal Service Quality with clients from various industries. Within TNS she is responsible for the development of TNS' offering in the area of Stakeholder Management, giving executive team advice and consulting clients globally on Stakeholder Management.

Introduction

Karin Jäger, TNS Infratest GmbH, joined TNS in 1986 and worked in several functions. In 1990 she developed the trade fair market research at TNS Infratest and was responsible for this area as a Director in the Stakeholder Management department until 2006, where she led continuous projects for Messe München GmbH. She now works in the Automotive sector as a division manager.

Chapter 7

Ian Jarvis worked for Burke / Infratest Burke / NFO / TNS for over 30 years! But over this time he has had 7 different jobs, including Managing Director and subsequently Chairman of Infratest Burke UK, and Managing Director of Infratest Burke International Services, responsible for the development of international research across the Group as it then was.

He worked with Jo Scharioth on the initial development of TRI*M, and latterly was a Director of the Global TRI*M Centre.

Chapter 1

Gudrun Kneissl heads the Market Research department at MAN Nutzfahrzeuge AG in Munich. She came to to MAN Group in 2006 and started at MAN Druckmaschinen AG heading the Market Intelligence department. From 1993 to 2005 she worked at TNS Infratest in different functions with her last position being Senior Consultant in the field of Stakeholder Management.

Chapter 3

Jens Krause, Graduate Economic Mathematician, has been working for TNS since 1996 and is a Director of Stakeholder Management with a focus on customer and employee surveys as well as Mystery Shopping. He is responsible for Software Development und Global Operations at the Global TRI*M Centre.

Chapter 12

Daniel Lindgren, TNS Indonesia, joined TNS in early 2002 and was head of polling and social research working closely with donor organizations such as UNICEF, IFES, ILO and IRI. In 2006, Daniel was placed in charge to set up the Stakeholder Management unit. He began his career in Sweden working for Esselte and Electrolux after which he moved to Australia to complete an MBA in Marketing. In Australia he held a number of managerial positions working with economic consulting, research and marketing within the finance industry.

Chapter 15

Dr. Susanne O'Gorman is Key Account Manager for Loyalty Partner and responsible for Knowledge Management at the Global TRI*M Centre. Currently she focuses on Customer Retention and the development of ISQ and Process Analysis. Before that she worked for over six year at TNS Infratest InCom as a director in the Telecommunications Market. Susanne did a degree in Sociology at the University of Regensburg. After a stay at the London School of Economics she finalised her PhD at the University of Regensburg.

Chapter 8

Dr. Peter Pirner is responsible for the business area Commercial Vehicles and works as sector champion for Stakeholder Management at TNS Infratest Automotive. Before that he worked as an international consulting executive for Stakeholder Management at the Global TRI*M Centre. Peter focused strongly on the development and marketing of the TRI*M business solution "Corporate Reputation Manager". Peter earned a PhD in Economics and a master in Business Administration from Munich University.

Chapter 9

Simon Priadko, Head of Market Research Department at VimpelCom Group, is responsible for the Group's market research in key business areas and geographies. He has more than 10 years of marketing and market research background at client and international MR institutes side. Simon is a strong supporter of Stakeholder Management principles in business and of the TRI*M model.

Chapter 14

Dr. Sandra Reich is Market Research Manager at MAN Nutzfahrzeuge AG and responsible for market research. Her focus is on international customer retention studies and the analysis of what drives purchase for commercial auto. After studying Business Administration with a focus on Marketing / Market Research at the university of Augsburg, she wrote her dissertation about the impact of advertising.

Chapter 9

Ulrich Sieber, Head of Human Resources Commerzbank, is responsible for Human Resources within Commerzbank Group. He started his banking career 25 years ago at Bayerische Vereinsbank, was trained in Corporate Banking and Human Resources and had several international stages. He studied Business Administration with a focus on Finance and Banking at Bankakademie in Munich and Frankfurt.

Chapter 10

Eric Sondervan is a Director of Business Solutions at TNS NIPO, Netherlands. Business Solutions are sophisticated research solutions for frequently occurring marketing problems to support companies to further strengthen their market position. Eric is an expert in Stakeholder Management and has developed many products in this areas of expertise in his research career of more than 20 years. He has a university degree in marketing & research from the University of Delft.

Chapter 4

Dr. Wolfgang Werner, Evonik AG, is responsible for projects in the area of Change Management at the headquarters of RAG in Essen. He leads employee surveys of Degussa. After studying Chemistry in Saarbrücken and Zurich, he gained a broad know-how in quality management, organisational development and internal management consulting in several chemical companies. He is also voluntarily working in the steering committee of DGQ, VCI and TÜV-Cert.

Chapter 11

Tim Zütphen studied Social Sciences and History in Bielefeld, Germany. He has been working for TNS since 1998 and is a Senior Consultant in the area of Stakeholder Management. He is also responsible for the Product Management of the Conversion Model.

Chapter 12

Scharioth, Joachim; **Huber,** Margit (Eds.)

**Achieving Excellence
in Stakeholder Management**

2003, VIII, 151 p. 44 illus., Hardcover
ISBN: 978-3-540-00255-0

Huber, Margit; **Scharioth,** Joachim;
Pallas, Martina (Eds.)

**Putting Stakeholder Management
into Practice**

2004, X, 174 p. 64 illus., Hardcover
ISBN: 978-3-540-20691-0

Huber, Margit; **Pallas,** Martina (Eds.)

**Customising Stakeholder
Management Strategies**
Concepts for Long-term Business Success

2006, XII, 139 p. 57 illus., Hardcover
ISBN: 978-3-540-31318-2